NORMAN CARR

Pioneer of Community-based Wildlife Conservation

ALISTAIR TOUGH

Gadsden Publishers

Gadsden Publishers
P.O. Box 32581, Lusaka, Zambia

Cover photograph courtesy of Judy Carr

ISBN: 978 9982 24 143 4

Dedication

Dedicated to Professor Michael Moss (1947-2021): mentor, colleague, hillwalking companion and badminton partner who encouraged me to continue work on this book when others questioned its value.

Table of Contents

List of Acronyms and Abbreviations

Acronym/abbreviation	Meaning
AG	Attorney General
ALC	African Lakes Corporation
ANC	African National Congress
BP	British Petroleum Company
DC	District Commissioner
GPHA	Game Preservation and Hunting Association
HMSO	Her / His Majesty's Stationery Office
HQ	Head Quarters
HRH	His Royal Highness
IMF	International Monetary Fund
K	Kwacha
KAR	King's African Rifles
KK	Kenneth Kaunda
LIRDP	Luangwa Integrated Resources Development Project
Lt-Col	Lieutenant-Colonel
MBE	Member of the Order of the British Empire
NCO	Non-Commissioned Officer
NHC	National Hotels Corporation
NPWS	National Parks and Wildlife Service
NRAMWU	Northern Rhodesia African Mine Workers Union
NRMWU	Northern Rhodesia Mine Workers Union
OPEC	Organisation of Oil Exporting Countries
POW	Prisoner(s) of War
SLNP	South Luangwa National Park
SRT	Save the Rhino Trust
SS	Steam Ship
UK	United Kingdom

UN	United Nations
UNIP	United National Independence Party
USA	United States of America
VIP	Very Important Person
WCSZ	Wildlife Conservation Society of Zambia
WWF	World Wildlife Fund, later World Wide Fund for Nature
ZNTB	Zambia National Tourist Board

Acknowledgements

First and foremost, I should like to give thanks to Judy Carr for her support and advice in preparing this biography of her father. Sadly, she did not live to see it published. I should like also to thank Mandy Shepherd, who spent time with Norman Carr over several decades. Several members of the Society of Malawi provided helpful inputs, most notably Pat Royale.

Several archivists, historians and librarians have had a role in enabling my research. I should like to thank the following, in particular: Bridget Howlett, Senior Archivist, London Metropolitan Archives; Dawn Sinclair, Archivist, Harper Collins; Dickson Vuwa Phiri and his colleagues in the Library of Chancellor College; Dora Wimbush, Librarian, Society of Malawi; Emmanuel Sianjani, Archivist, National Archives of Zambia; Lucy McCann, Archivist, Bodleian Library of Commonwealth and Africa Studies at Rhodes House, Oxford; Michael Moss, Research Professor, University of Glasgow; Michael Palmer, Archivist, Zoological Society of London; Paul Lihoma, Director of the National Records and Archives Service, Malawi; Rosalind Pulvermacher, FCO Historical Branch; and my former colleagues in Archives and Special Collections at the University of Glasgow. For advice on the process of publication, I should like to thank James Fleming, Sir John Lister-Kaye, Neil McCallum, and Richard Stenlake, and, above all, my publisher, Fay Gadsden. Nikki Ashley deserves especial thanks for editing the final manuscript and removing inconsistencies that had crept in during a long and much interrupted period of writing.

I should also like to pay tribute to those who first interested me in African history: Dr Roy Bridges and Professor John Hargreaves, both of Aberdeen University; and Professor Andrew Roberts of the School of Oriental and African Studies in London.

Chapter 1

Childhood and School

Introduction

Today Norman Carr is remembered for his work as a conservationist in Zambia. Norman pioneered community-based conservation in Africa in the 1940s, when he persuaded Chief Nsefu to create a game reserve in Zambia's Luangwa Valley. To begin with Nsefu was sceptical – he asked why people who had nice houses in towns would want to come into the bush? Carr had a good understanding of the realities of life for villagers and he knew that the cost of creating conventional national parks fell particularly on villagers who lost their land and opportunities to hunt for meat. So, Norman's idea was for a reserve run by local people who would benefit from the entrance fees paid by visitors.

Norman pioneered another innovation in the Luangwa Valley – walking safaris. These involved visitors walking and sleeping out in the bush, providing a more equal relationship between human beings and wildlife than can be achieved from sitting passively in a four-wheel drive vehicle. During the 1950s Norman became concerned about habitat degradation. He advocated culling on the grounds that success in conservation depended on the defence of the habitat, rather than the protection of individual animals. Nonetheless, he was a founder of the Save the Rhino Trust which campaigned against the commercial extermination of the rhinoceros.

Norman spent the formative years of his life in Malawi, except for ten years at school in the UK. His experiences in Malawi had a profound influence on him and that is where this account must begin.

Early Life

Norman Joseph Carr was born in the British Concession at Chinde on the East African coast on 19 July 1912. His father, Ernest Alfred Carr, is known to have been working in Central Africa for Kellers Ltd. from 1898 and had moved to Chinde in 1900 to work for the African Lakes Corporation (ALC). It is possible that Ernest's roots in Africa went deeper: the records of the African Lakes Corporation refer to a Mr Carr working for them twenty years before, but no indisputable evidence exists to show that that Mr Carr was related to Ernest.

Chinde stands beside a shallow mouth of the River Zambezi in what was then called Portuguese East Africa (now Mozambique). Goods and passengers travelling to and from the landlocked protectorate of British Central Africa (later Nyasaland and now Malawi) passed through Chinde and then up the navigable stretches of the Zambezi and Shire rivers to a railway terminus, originally Port Herald (Nsanje) in Southern Nyasaland and later Chindio in Portuguese territory. The Chinde branch of the Zambezi delta led into a natural canal through which shallow vessels could pass. Here they were sheltered from bad weather in the Indian Ocean by the sandy promontory on which the British Concession stood. Ocean-going ships stood some miles offshore whilst passengers and goods were transferred into shallow lighters, which were then towed into the Chinde channel. Shallow-draft steamers with paddle wheels fastened to their sterns were used for the journey up-river. First class passengers travelled in the paddle steamers whilst steerage passengers and most freight travelled in the holds of lighters lashed alongside. In Chinde there were bonded warehouses in which goods in transit could be stored without paying customs duties to the Portuguese authorities. The Head Postmaster of Nyasaland was resident in Chinde and all post from or to post offices in British Central Africa passed through Chinde. This made Chinde an ideal base for the African Lakes Corporation's import-export business which included placing orders for goods (often from Britain or South Africa) on behalf of planters and traders and then ensuring that the goods were despatched intact to their customers.

Ernest Carr began work for the African Lakes Corporation as a clerk. His duties included managing accounts and checking the waybills and other paperwork associated with the transportation and distribution of goods. As a single man he lived in the African Lakes Corporation's hotel, a hostel housing about up to eight expatriate staff. Facilities in the hotel included a piano and a billiards table. Over time Ernest's skills were expanded, his duties became more demanding, and his salary increased substantially. He became skilled in making valuations, qualified as a surveyor, and took on responsibility for managing the ALC's fleet of paddle steamers and lighters. During the First World War, the volume of business was high, both with soldiers travelling up country from Chinde, and the handling of large quantities of war materiel.

Norman's mother, formerly Miss Emily Joseph, had come out to South Africa in 1902. Passenger lists for the SS Walmer Castle show that Emily had travelled from Britain to Port Elizabeth with her parents and siblings. Presumably, Ernest and Emily met in South Africa. They married in London in January 1910 whilst Ernest was on home leave. Emily and Ernest arrived together in Chinde on 2nd March 1910. Ernest and Emily Carr appear to have been well-off financially. They lived in a two-storey house (one of only two in Chinde) and this gave them the full benefit of offshore breezes in the morning and onshore breezes in the late afternoon. It also reduced the irritations caused by mosquitoes and other insects by raising their living quarters well above ground level. Family photographs show Ernest and Emily being carried in a machila, a hammock suspended beneath a stout pole with a sunshade fitted overhead. Norman was the second of four children: his sister Evelyn was a year older whilst his brother Alan was seven years younger and Cecily was the baby of the family.

Passengers travelling up-country usually spent a few nights in Murray's Hotel in Chinde. The Carrs were acquainted with many of the travellers and well known for their hospitality. The Nyasaland Times stated in their obituary of Ernest that he was renowned for his hospitality and kindness everywhere. At Chinde he was known amongst the Portuguese as 'the man with the ever-open door'.' Norman remembered that as a small boy he was thrilled by the conversations of big game hunters who frequently spent the evenings on the cool balcony of his parents' home, and he later said that these overheard conversations created in him a great ambition to become a hunter himself. Norman recalled also that it was his mother's habit to take him and his sister to the beach in the later afternoon, once the full heat of the sun had passed. The family had access to the ALC's tennis courts and would presumably have used these in the cooler hours of the day also. The Carrs' neighbours and particular friends were the Bishop family. Alexander Bishop represented the British Central Africa Company at Chinde where, like Ernest Carr, he kept the accounts and managed their river fleet. The Bishops had many children and they, too, enjoyed playing on the beach. In addition, the Bishop family regularly hosted musical evenings with convivial singing. Mrs Lillian Bishop wrote about this part of her life, saying:

> Granted the heat and mosquitoes were pretty bad, and we had no fresh flowers, vegetables or milk. But we did have the beach and the sea and sufficient congenial company for a happy social life. … One great boon, which many people today will envy, was the great variety of fish we got … including crabs, and oysters and prawns … There were only a few grocer shops at Chinde, but occasionally, especially at Christmas time, we went out by tug to a big liner where we did our shopping …[1]

Presumably, there would have been ample fresh tropical fruit available at Chinde.

Whilst Norman enjoyed his childhood in Chinde, it was a place that some travellers disliked. Mary Bridson, who travelled via Chinde to Zomba to visit the Governor, Sir Alfred Sharpe, wrote 'Chinde, however, is bad even for an African port … a small collection of tin houses on a sandbank'.[2] In addition, Chinde was exposed to particularly bad tropical storms sweeping in from the Indian Ocean. One storm in February 1918 lasted for three days and caused extensive damage. Norman's vivid description of a storm at Chinde is worth quoting at length:

> Suddenly the skies opened and the rain poured down in a solid flood. Blinding flashes of lightning exploded simultaneously with every crash of thunder and between each salvo a continuous rumble could be heard … The force of the wind … built up until the crescendo of noise was unendurable – high pitched like a human shriek. Giant hands seemed to push our house, causing it to sway drunkenly … I cannot remember seeing my father at all during the whole episode, but I suppose that like all other able-bodied men, he was out in the boats doing rescue and salvage work all day.[3]

It seems clear that Norman was born with one physiological feature that would prove an advantage in later life. His body produced an above-average amount of melanin and this became evident because he had brown eyes. In people of European descent, high levels of melanin result in the development of a deep suntan rather than sunburn. In addition, Norman could go out in the harsh African sun without needing sunglasses or a broad-brimmed hat because of his brown eyes.

School Days

Norman was sent away to school in the UK in February 1920. His first school was Ryde House Commercial School in Ripley, Surrey, a long-established boarding school with a reputation for cricket. He remained there until 1927. It was probably during this period that his parents received a school report stating that their son set himself low standards which he failed to achieve. In October 1927, aged 15, he moved to Clark's College in London. This had originally served as a 'crammer' for those preparing to sit civil service examinations. In the Edwardian era the founder, George E. Clark, decided to add what was then called a 'Modern School'. This was a secondary school which trained boys aged 11 and above to become clerks, civil servants, and business administrators. At Ryde House and Clark's College, Norman learned shorthand, typing, bookkeeping and business practice, passing the London Chamber of Commerce Certificate for Handwriting with distinction. Clearly his parents intended Norman to have a commercial career. Quite possibly his father envisaged Norman joining him in the import-export business at Chinde. This may explain why Norman later wrote that he had not achieved scholarly distinction whilst at school, for the schools he attended did not concern themselves with the ornamental forms of scholarship, such as Latin and Ancient Greek. During his final year at Clark's College, Norman was head prefect, and captain of both the cricket and football teams. As head prefect he would have been entitled - and expected - to inflict corporal punishment on junior pupils for minor breaches of discipline. That he did not misuse this power would have been regarded by contemporaries as a key indicator of 'character' and suitability to hold positions of responsibility. That Clark's College pupils played soccer rather than rugby may be significant, as this distinction was a line of demarcation between the lower-middle classes and the upper-middle classes.

Whilst Norman was studying at Clark's College he lived at 23 Forest View Road, Walthamstow in East London. Walthamstow, as a respectable commuter suburb of London, had developed between 1870 and 1890 with the coming of the railways. The Nyasaland Times described Emily Carr as coming from Walthamstow, so presumably 23 Forest View Road was the home of Norman's grandparents, or some other relatives on his mother's side.

Norman did not see his parents at any time during his schooling. It is possible that he spent many of the vacations at the home of a W. Jones in Westcliff-on-Sea in Essex. At any rate, when applying for a job in 1931 he named Mr Jones as a personal referee and indicated that Jones had known him throughout his time in the UK.

It was not uncommon for the children of the British Empire to spend long periods separated from their parents. Most, however, did visit or receive visits at least once every three or four years. So, it is worth considering why Norman saw nothing of Ernest and Emily between February 1920 and January 1929. The explanation lies principally in the declining fortunes of the British Concession at Chinde.

Norman's Parents in Africa

On 24 February 1922 a cyclone struck Chinde. This was the worst storm for at least thirty years. Most buildings had their roofs blown off. Many of the bonded warehouses were inundated. At the double-storied home of the Carr family, water covered the floors on the upper level to a depth of two feet. Meanwhile the paddle steamers, barges, and lighters on which Chinde depended for its existence had suffered badly. Many were sunk. When the storm abated and water levels returned to normal it was found that many of the surviving vessels were over a mile inland. The Trans-Zambezi Railway Company saw their opportunity and bought up the remaining paddle steamers – without which it would be impossible for Chinde to compete with the railways.

Ernest and Emily Carr had lost their home and their livelihood. Whilst the goods in transit in the bonded warehouses were covered by maritime insurance, domestic premises were covered under separate insurance policies and these excluded 'Acts of God'. So, the furniture, furnishings and clothing destroyed by the cyclone were uninsured. Ernest and Emily relocated to Blantyre, the commercial capital of Nyasaland (as British Central Africa was then called). They had a good network of contacts, and it was reasonable to expect that Ernest would be able to develop a new and successful business there. He did, at least, have accumulated capital to make a start. The ALC had sought to retain staff in 1917 and 1918 by promising a retention bonus on salaries. In 1917 this had been promised at the rate of ten per cent, but late in 1918, when the company's profits were exceptionally high, the directors increased the bonus to thirty per cent. So, Ernest set out to make a fresh start with money in the bank.

According to Norman, his father's capacity for putting trust in people who either lacked business acumen or were intrinsically untrustworthy led to a series of financial setbacks. One such transaction led to a court case and from the legal records it is possible to get some notion of Ernest's difficulties. In June 1928 he sold a Ford truck on a hire purchase basis to Suleman Abdul Karim. The total sum due was £100 of which Karim paid only £38 (of which £30 was the initial down payment). In April 1929 Ernest took Karim to the courts and got the truck back. The key point here is that Karim's defence lawyer could have argued that the hire purchase agreement was void because it contravened the Credit Trade with Natives Ordinance of 1926. The Credit Trade law existed to protect unsophisticated African people from exploitation by European traders. Ernest Carr was fortunate that the judge decided that law did not apply to Karim as he was of mixed race. Nonetheless, this episode may have damaged Ernest's reputation as a businessman because he had made questionable judgments in respect of Karim and the law. It is not clear whether similar factors came into play in respect of Ernest's unsuccessful venture into tobacco farming in the 1920s. In partnership with W. James he farmed the Mpemba Estate which is situated about ten miles from the centre of Blantyre on the road to Chikwawa. It is possible that the soil and climate, rather than the selection of an unsuitable business partner, were the key factors in the failure of this venture. At some point in the 1920s, Ernest returned to a more familiar line of business by establishing the Nyasaland Auctioneering, Commission and Insurance Agency in Blantyre.

Given the financial stresses to which Norman's parents were subjected, it is easy for an adult to understand that simply paying their son's school fees represented a major achievement. This is unlikely to have been evident to a small boy stranded thousands of miles away. It is significant that one of Norman's favourite books during his time at Ryde House was Rudyard Kipling's *The Jungle Book*. In the book Mowgli, a small boy, is abandoned in a dark and frightening jungle by his parents. Overcoming fear Mowgli survives and eventually flourishes in the jungle. Ultimately, he returns to his parents' village to find them in danger and rescues them. The appeal of this story for Norman and thousands of other boys in his position is obvious. But he could not have foreseen how prophetic the closing part of the 'Jungle book' story would be.

Chapter 2

Poacher turned Record Keeper

In January 1929 Norman Carr set out from London to return to his family in Africa. The journey took him through the port of Beira where he caught the sleeper train to Blantyre. The train departed late in the afternoon, in order to avoid the worst of the day's heat. In the hottest months, between October and March, the compartments would have been stifling despite this precaution. The train remained at low altitude for hundreds of miles and only climbed up onto the Shire Highlands plateau once it had passed the confluence of the Ruo and Shire rivers. Then it rose gradually on the eastern side of the Mulanje Massif. As a small child he had travelled up the Zambezi and Shire rivers in a paddle steamer. The train was quicker and had the advantage that it did not periodically run aground.

There are two differing, but not necessarily incompatible versions of what Norman did for a living once he reached Blantyre. In his autobiographical writings he has described how he devoted much time to hunting, both legally in Nyasaland and illegally in Portuguese East Africa. In a job application submitted in 1931 he makes no reference to hunting at all. Instead, he refers to his father's business, the Nyasaland Auctioneering, Commission and Insurance Agency as his employer and describes his duties as 'Keeping complete accounts, books, balance sheets [and] correspondence, shorthand and typewriting.'

The apparent inconsistency is not too difficult to explain. His father would have been happy to give Norman work to do, even though Norman felt that the relationship between them was never really intimate after their ten years of separation. However, following the Wall Street Crash of October 1929, the economy of Nyasaland had shrunk rapidly. Those traders who remained in business had reduced their stock whilst most planters deferred capital investment. So, there was only a limited amount of work for Norman to do in his father's ailing business. This provided

Norman with a great opportunity to pursue the dream he had nurtured throughout his school days in Britain, to become a big game hunter. In Nyasaland, he worked for the government as a part-time crop protector on a piecework basis. In theory he and others like him were supposed to watch over villagers' vegetable gardens until elephants raided them, then follow the offending animals and shoot them. According to Norman neither he nor any of his counterparts were willing to sit around for weeks waiting for an elephant to raid a garden. Instead, he followed and shot any elephant that he encountered. Even if this was not especially effective as a technique for protecting crops (as the elephants shot might not be crop raiders at all) it was still popular with villagers to whom it delivered a windfall supply of meat. Norman was permitted to take and sell one tusk from each animal killed. However, in Portuguese East Africa Norman operated as a poacher pure and simple. He later wrote that knowing he risked punishment if caught simply added to the excitement. He wrote also about the great enthusiasm that he shared with other young and inexperienced hunters like himself and how they often sat up late into the night talking about game animals and hunting. There may have been another reason for him to feel excited about his trips into the bush. Villagers who received large presents of meat customarily rewarded African hunters with the sexual favours of a particularly pretty girl. It is possible, but not certain, that Norman would have been accorded the same reward. He wrote many years later about the practice, recalling that the fundi (expert African hunters) referred to their honorary wives as 'spare tyres'. And Barbara Carr described in one of her books how she noticed that the village elders might have a plump young woman with unusually large breasts available when European civil servants were around.

On his twentieth birthday, 19th July 1932, Norman shot his fiftieth elephant. This equates to a kill rate of about one per month over two and a half years. By then, however, Norman's life had taken a new and unanticipated path. In February 1931 Ernest Carr encouraged his older son to apply for the post of junior clerk in the government of Nyasaland which would entail moving to the colonial capital in Zomba about forty miles away from Blantyre. Norman completed an application form in which he claimed two years' relevant working experience and a working knowledge of the main African language used in the area, Chi-Manyanja (now known as Chichewa in Malawi and Cinyanja in neighbouring Zambia). He supplied an excellent testimonial from the principal of Clark's College. In addition, a confidential reference was supplied by A. J. Stone, Registrar and Administrator-General at the High Court in Blantyre, stating 'I know Carr Jr. socially and can say he is a gentlemanly young fellow and unassuming although half his athletic abilities has been the cause of swollen heads in others. I confidently recommend him to you.' Stone added that the training provided by Clark's College was '... first class for adaptability in any office ...'.

To describe Norman Carr's experience as a civil servant, and development as a young adult, it is necessary to put it into context. This involves a detailed description of methods of administration and social conventions.

Norman's first month as a clerk was spent in the district commissioner's office in Zomba, known locally as 'the boma'. The boma was - and still is - located on the main road through Zomba which comes from the direction of Blantyre and heads towards Lake Nyasa (Lake Malawi) via the Liwonde crossing of the Shire River. The district commissioner, or DC, at the time was Mr A. C. Kirby. Kirby was in his early forties and had passed the civil service examinations in law at the higher level. After studying at Balliol College, Oxford he had joined the colonial service in Kenya in 1913 (the year after Norman's birth) and transferred to Nyasaland in 1925. On paper there was an assistant district officer, Mr R. H. Keppel-Compton, but Norman would not have worked alongside him as Keppel-Compton had been seconded to the Secretariat as a temporary executive officer: the significance of this detail is explained below. In May 1932 Norman moved to the Secretariat, up on the slopes of Zomba Mountain, to work for the Attorney General, or AG. The AG was the chief law officer of the Crown and as such the government's main legal adviser. The AG at the time was Mr (later Sir) Walter Harragin who was in his early forties and had served in Trinidad before transferring to Nyasaland. The AG's work involved considering the constitutionality of proposed legislation, the legality of policy under consideration, and the advisability of bringing high-profile court cases in the name of the government. It was very sensitive work. The AG was assisted by two assistant attorney generals. These were: Captain Lancelot Lloyd-Blood who had studied at Trinity College Dublin and then been an army officer during the First World War, and who had been awarded the Military Cross, before serving in Kenya and then transferring to Nyasaland; and Mr Rupert Haig who had studied at Glenalmond School and Brasenose College, Oxford. Haig was only a few years older than Norman and had commenced his colonial service in Nyasaland just three years before. Norman's job consisted largely of typing the AG's and assistant AGs' handwritten drafts of documents, searching for precedents (i.e. previous decisions on matters similar to the current case) and of maintaining the record keeping system. The record keeping included making entries in a 'precedent book', so that in future consistent decisions would be possible, and creating entries in registers and a card index. In order to do these things, it was necessary that Norman should read every document being placed in the record keeping system. It was essential also that he keep what he learnt to himself. Any indiscrete gossiping could have cost him his job and that would have been catastrophic for his family.

Soon after Norman entered government service, his father died. Shortly before his death, Ernest Carr had devoted several days and nights to nursing his old friend from Chinde, Alexander Bishop. Bishop died of pneumonia on 26th May 1931, and it seems likely that Ernest's death on 3 June was caused by the same disease. Mrs Emily Carr was left virtually penniless. Her husband's business - the Nyasaland Auctioneering, Commission and Insurance Agency - was almost worthless and their savings had been lost in unsuccessful business ventures, including a tobacco farm. In the depths of the Great Depression, she was not alone in facing hard times. Her younger son, Alan, was only 13 and still at school in Britain. Her daughter Cecily was even younger than Alan. Norman took on the full responsibility for maintaining his mother and younger siblings. Mrs Emily Carr relocated from Blantyre to Zomba and kept house for Norman there.

Norman Carr had joined the civil service as a local recruit without the leave privileges given to more senior men recruited in Britain. His starting salary was £185 per year plus a £50 housing allowance. This made him the lowest paid European in the civil service. It also placed him on the lowest rung of an elaborate social hierarchy ladder. As an 'un-established' clerk he had no job security and no pension entitlement. Norman's name, rank and salary were published in the Government List along with the same details in respect of all European civil servants and military officers. The Government List was a quarterly publication. The African Lakes Corporation and all other major trading companies had copies and used the information on salaries to fix the credit that might be given to customers who worked in the civil service. The credit available to Emily Carr would have been determined by her son's earnings as she was keeping house for him. The staff list was used also to determine where guests should sit at dinner parties that were hosted and attended by civil servants. Norman's place would have been at the outermost margins of any dining table in Zomba. Shortly after becoming a civil servant, he would have had to attend two such dinners: one hosted by the governor and another hosted by the chief secretary who was head of the civil service. Custom required that Norman should have visiting cards printed. He then had to 'call' on the governor and the chief secretary by visiting their official residences and leaving his card. At Government House, where the governor lived, there was a tray kept beside the sentry box for this purpose. Then invitations to dinner would arrive and Norman would have to attend. For young officers, even those who had been educated at famous public schools and universities, this could be an ordeal. For Norman it must have been a cause of great anxiety, lest he cause offence. Mercifully, there was no requirement that reciprocal invitations to dine should be sent by unmarried junior officers to their seniors.

For seven years Norman worked in the Secretariat, the centre of government. Here it was expected that he would wear khaki shorts, a shirt and tie and long socks – the customary outfit for lower ranking colonial officials. He started work at 7 o'clock in the morning and worked until noon. There was then a two-hour break for lunch, during which most officials went home, followed by a two hours stint between 2 o'clock and 4 o'clock. The time between 4 o'clock and sunset at about 5.45 p.m. was customarily devoted to sporting activities. The Gymkhana Club had tennis courts and a hockey / soccer pitch and there was a rather steeply inclined golf course on the lower slopes of Zomba Mountain. The Secretariat Building where Norman worked was on two floors. Upstairs were the offices of the chief secretary and the principal technical officers – the director of agriculture, the director of public works, the director of medical services, the postmaster general, the attorney general and so on. On this level were kept the confidential records of government. Some of these were in the AG's office but the greater part was in a Confidential Registry. This was attached to the Chief Secretary's Office but used as a shared resource by all the principal technical officers. After a period of work in the AG's office, Norman was regarded as competent and trustworthy and was moved to the Confidential Registry. Downstairs was a much larger Open Registry in which records were kept that were not considered confidential. This was staffed by African clerks who were generally regarded by British personnel as being inefficient: some European civil servants attributed this to poor pay. It was in the Open Registry that the post and telegrams were sent and received.

In the Secretariat there were a number of district commissioners who had been brought in from outlying areas to serve as temporary executive officers, including Mr Keppel-Compton from the Zomba boma. Characteristically the DCs had been educated at Repton, Rugby, Haileybury or other well-known British public schools. Many, including Keppel-Compton, had studied at Oxford or Cambridge. They often were attracted to the Colonial Administrative Service because an outdoor life, involving high levels of responsibility at an early age appealed to them. They were usually capable of decision-making, possessed of physical strength and courage and assumed a natural air of authority. By the time they were posted to the Secretariat most were over the age of thirty. Many of them had received a classical education and would quote from Latin and Ancient Greek literature in the course of everyday conversation. It would have been odd if Norman had not felt a little over-awed in their company. This was accentuated by their respective roles. The DC executive officers were in the Secretariat to express their opinions. They were given official papers to read and were expected to follow a process known as 'minuting up'. This meant that the DCs offered opinions and advice on a range of topics to senior technical officers. Those who received the advice might then consult the AG or the chief secretary or even the governor before deciding on a course of action. Frequently, once a decision was made, instructions would be given to the executive officers to write a letter, a report, or memorandum: as they did so they would learn whether their opinions had been heeded. Most DCs freely admitted that they did not find this work congenial. Kenneth Bradley has written about his time in the Secretariat in Northern Rhodesia in the 1920s and 1930s:

> I now spent my days trying to be intelligent about problems which I did not understand because they lay outside my own experience, such as schemes for scientific research, and such educational mysteries as 'middle' and 'normal' schools....Yet whenever business took me to the offices of the local District Commissioner and I saw the quiet groups of African villagers sitting under the trees awaiting their turn to talk to him, my heart turned over. There was a real Africa out there beyond the files and telephone wires and I must get back to it.[4]

However, promotion to the rank of provincial commissioner, chief secretary and possibly governor was only open to those DCs who had served satisfactorily in the Secretariat. Norman's role was in stark contrast. He was there to register documents, create index cards, make entries in precedent books, and type confidential documents. Emphatically, he was not expected to offer opinions. At the outset, Norman's work was unnecessarily onerous because the Secretariat in Zomba had not followed the lead given by many other British colonies in moving over to an up-to-date filing system. In places such as Trinidad, Mauritius, Zanzibar, and Northern Rhodesia the record-keeping systems operated on the principle of one file, one subject. Related papers were drawn together in a single file and managed as one unit. This significantly reduced the amount of drudgery associated with record keeping. In Zomba, however, they continued with an antique system in which each letter, report and memorandum was managed as a separate unit and therefore complex card indices and cross-referencing systems had to be maintained. Governor Sir George Smith had tried to change this immediately after the First World War, but two successive Chief Secretaries, Sir Hector Duff and Mr Robert Rankine had tenaciously clung to the outdated methods with which they were familiar. During the period that Norman was working in the Confidential Registry it was reorganised as a modern filing system. Who took that decision is not clear. However, as the clerk in charge of the registry, Norman would have had the mammoth task of creating a filing system that reflected the business methods and functions of the colonial system. This insider knowledge was to prove valuable later in his career.

A curious aspect of Norman's delicate relationship with his colleagues arose because Norman maintained - and thus had access to - personnel (i.e. Human Resources) records including the confidential reports that were compiled every year on each European civil servant. So, if the director of medical services wrote that the district medical officer in Port Herald might be developing an opium addiction then Norman knew this was the case but was honour-bound to say nothing about it to anyone. Similarly, if the provincial commissioner wrote that the assistant DC at Zomba, Mr Keppel-Compton, was believed to have marital problems then Norman knew that too.

Given the potentially difficult social relationships that living and working in Zomba could produce, it is hardly surprising that Norman chose to spend many of his weekends in the bush. This did not inhibit his mother. Emily Carr was an active member of the Gymkhana Club where she could play whist, and have access through the Club's library to magazines and books that would otherwise have been unaffordable. Once each week, there was a cinema night. As Norman took his car with him into the bush, his mother routinely walked home in the dark even though lions were still prowling the streets of Zomba at this time. In the bush, Norman honed his fieldcraft skills and his ability to follow and interpret an animal's tracks. Through his hunting he was able to supplement his income with the proceeds from selling ivory and this was a pattern that persisted into his married life. His brother Alan, once his schooldays were over, became a regular companion on Norman's hunting trips. The two brothers travelled in an Austin Tourer car which they customised for use in the bush. Their usual pattern was to set off early on Friday evening or Saturday morning and return on Sunday evening.

They both joined the Nyasaland Volunteers, an auxiliary unit of the British army. Norman joined in Blantyre in 1929. The Nyasaland Volunteers was a slightly curious organisation. In wartime its members would be expected to serve as officers, or senior non-commissioned officers, in battalions made up primarily of African recruits. In peacetime, however, they served as privates in an entirely European force. This gave them a chance to escape from the delays and frustrations that were commonplace in working with alien peoples and cultures and spend time in the company of their fellow countrymen. This desire to spend weekends with one's peers was not unique: the Inns of Court Yeomanry, a unit made up of London lawyers who preferred their peacetime soldiering to be amongst their friends and colleagues, was similar to the Nyasaland Volunteers. Ernest Carr had served in the Nyasaland Volunteers, and Norman's future father-in-law was a member too. It seems to have had at its core a group of men who had been sergeants or even sergeant-majors in the regular army before entering the colonial service. Jack Archer the Superintendent of Prisons of the Nyasaland government was a leading figure in the Nyasaland Volunteers. Archer had been a regimental sergeant major in the regular army, and he would have ensured that the standards of drill (i.e. marching in formation on parade) were as high as those on the rifle range.

In addition to his weekend soldiering, Norman continued to play cricket occasionally: he appeared in annual matches between the civil service and the settler population which took place over two days in May each year.

As Norman spent many Sundays in the bush, he cannot have been a regular worshipper at Zomba's Anglican Church. Writing many years later, he did refer to praying whilst in the bush. His wife recalled that their irregular attendance at church puzzled Mateyu, a long-serving member of her domestic staff of whom more will be said later. In some colonial capitals, absence from Sunday worship might have damaged a junior official's career prospects. Norman was fortunate in this respect. Firstly, because the Anglican bishop had his cathedral on distant Likoma Island and therefore a ceremonial attendance by the governor with his officials assembled in order of precedence was not a feature of life in Zomba as it was in Lusaka and many other colonial capitals. Secondly, because the Anglican Church in Zomba was smaller than its Presbyterian counterpart as many of the senior officials were Scots. So, it was easy for Norman to absent himself from church without drawing adverse attention.

Norman's early years in the Secretariat must have been anxious ones. The government deferred the process of moving him onto the permanent staff (which would entitle him to a pension on retirement) because the financial situation in the depths of the worldwide depression was so bad. Nonetheless, in January 1933 his salary was increased by £15 to £201 per annum and he received further £15 raises in salary in 1934, 1935, and 1936. Ultimately, his good service was rewarded. Norman was an intelligent and capable clerk, well able to cope with his work, and he demonstrated qualities of discretion and trustworthiness that were highly valued by his superiors. On 14th August 1935 he was enrolled in the government's non-contributory pension scheme and given credit for previous service. As his future wife Barbara testified in her books, this was a major matter for Norman, whose father had only been saved from an impoverished old age by premature death: Norman was eager to avoid the same fate. From April 1936 Norman was promoted from junior clerk to clerk and his salary was increased to £300 per year: by 1939 this had risen to £336 which represented a substantial improvement on his £186 starting salary.

Barbara Carr described the impact that working with confidential record-keeping systems had on those carrying it out in the Secretariat in Lusaka in the 1940s.

> They were so used to dealing with people's lives on paper that they seemed to have lost contact with the world of reality. They were pillars of discretion and models of secrecy. They knew so

> much about everybody and were embedded in their loyalty to
> such a degree that they seemed to have lost the power of ordinary
> speech, as if they were afraid that they might say something they
> shouldn't.[5]

That Norman was not subject to the worst extremes of this kind of psychological damage may be attributed to a range of factors. Most importantly, in his sporting achievements, in his hunting and in his Nyasaland Volunteers activities he displayed a kind of masculinity that was admired by his colleagues and sustaining to his self-esteem.

Chapter 3

Elephant Control and Military Service, 1939-43

Crop Protection: Luangwa Valley

The government of Northern Rhodesia (Zambia) appointed Norman Carr as a game ranger in July 1939. His main job was to protect the crops of local African farmers from wild animals. Until November he was based in Fort Jameson (Chipata) and responsible for the huge Eastern Province, including the Luangwa Valley. In practice, Norman's work consisted overwhelmingly of shooting elephants. Baboons, bushpigs and hippos raided vegetable gardens also, but they were much less readily controlled by means of shooting. Elephants, on the other hand, seemed to be capable of learning from the experience of others: if some crop raiders were shot in one area and other elephants were left in peace to graze on their natural diet in another area then the population would tend to congregate around the second area.

Norman was given this new job both because of his record as a weekend hunter and his track record as a clerk. The acting governor of Nyasaland commended him as a reliable and conscientious civil servant. This created resentment amongst the big game hunters living in the Fort Jameson area, some of whom had applied for the job. They regarded him as a jumped-up, pen-pushing youngster. One of their number known to the local people as Bwana Chiduli (Mr Short-cut) even went on a spree of poaching to demonstrate his contempt for the new game ranger. Norman was neither able to catch Bwana Chiduli nor to discover his true identity. His response to this situation was to push himself to the limit of his endurance to demonstrate his true worth. Between the months of July and November of 1939, Norman shot 200 crop raiding elephants – often at a rate of three per day. This silenced his critics.

Norman's area of operations was divided between the South Luangwa Game Reserve and the rest of the Valley. The Game Reserve covered a large area on the river's west bank. Here shooting wild animals was prohibited and it was Norman's duty to prevent poaching. The Game Reserve had been created in the first decade of the twentieth century when there was an autonomous government of North Eastern Rhodesia (now the eastern part of Zambia) based in Fort Jameson. At this time, there was concern that the animal population had been much reduced by commercial hunting. During the 1880s and 1890s the African Lakes Company had bought large quantities of ivory sourced from the Luangwa Valley which was sold to it by Swahili traders who the ALC described as 'Senga Arabs'. As a result, the elephant population was believed to be much reduced. The giraffe population was very small also. In fact, the steady growth of the giraffe population was one of the real achievements of the Game Reserve. When the Game Reserve was declared, the small government outpost at Fort Hargreaves which stood inside the Reserve's boundaries was closed. One of the staff based there had been Thornicroft, the man who first identified Thornicroft's Giraffe as a separate sub-species.

We have vivid descriptions of the Luangwa Valley and the surrounding area that were written in 1938 by Kenneth Bradley, the district officer based in Fort Jameson. Bradley who, as Sir Kenneth, was later to become the director of the Imperial Institute in London, loved to get out of his office and go on *ulendo* (safari) in the rural districts. Setting out for the Luangwa in July he wrote in his diary 'The prospect of a journey into the valley … thrills me to my boots'.[6] Once in the Valley he added:

> Dawn … here the mist glowed, the green lightened, the sand and the papyrus plumes began to shine… After breakfast we broke camp and … we climbed … from the bank into the deep forest. A fearsome place. It was very silent. One felt that it was dangerous; that it was teeming with sinister life: giant snakes, buffalo, lion, and elephant … there was spoor enough but we met nothing … the tsetse-fly came out to feed. I think that they must have observed a fast yesterday, knowing that we were coming… It was a relief to come out of the forest again into the gardens of the next group of villages. The people complained bitterly of the ravages of baboon and elephant. Their crops had been ruined. But I noticed enough beer brewing .[7]

Bradley noted that even worse than the tsetse fly was the buffalo bean which released clouds of microscopic hairs causing 'the most awful irritation possible to conceive' for which the only remedy was a mud bath.[8] Like Norman Carr, Kenneth Bradley reckoned that the natural beauty of the Valley more than compensated for the discomforts involved in being there. He expressed this in terms that showed remarkable awareness of his time and place:

> ... until I came here I had never before met man in fief to the wild. As far as I can see, the more formidable animals of the Luangwa take about as much notice of a human being as we do of a beetle. It would be a lesson to the human race ... if the situation were more common.[9]

In the Luangwa Valley, Bradley and other colonial officers had a particularly good relationship with Chief Sefu (Nsefu) of the Kunda people. When Achewa tribal leaders had tried to persuade some villagers to transfer their allegiance from Nsefu to an Achewa chief, Bradley had been resolute in refusing to allow this. Nsefu had reciprocated by encouraging his people to grow cash crops in accordance with a marketing scheme promoted by the provincial commissioner. Over time Chief Nsefu developed a reputation with the colonial government as a progressive chief. By 1949 Nsefu's standing was so high that he was introduced to Arthur Creech-Jones, the British cabinet minister responsible for the colonies, when Creech-Jones arrived at Fort Jameson airport.

Norman's work as a crop protector had, of necessity, to be concentrated on the season of the year when the main grain crops were growing and being harvested. This was the rainy season. It is difficult to convey to anyone who has not seen it with their own eyes what the rains are like in Central Africa. In the 1930s and 1940s there was a pattern that repeated itself every year, except for one drought year in the late 1940s. At the onset of the rains, usually in late October or early November, atmospheric pressure built up and temperatures rose. Then a day came when the heavens opened, and vast quantities of water fell rapidly. Instantly a wonderful earthy aroma rose from the ground and anyone who was not under shelter was soaked in a matter of seconds. After the first rains the earth absorbed most of the water and plant growth luxuriated. Crops, wild grass, creepers, shrubs and trees burst into life and grew rapidly. Within a few weeks a pattern became evident:

> each afternoon the clouds gathered until around 4 o'clock rain fell heavily for an hour or so. Then the sun emerged, the sky cleared and anyone standing on a hill could see for miles. But in the Luangwa Valley the grass grew to such a height and in such profusion that visibility at ground level was often only a few feet. Swiftly the ground became saturated. Water courses that had been filled with dust became rivers. Rivers became torrents. Slight depressions known as *dambos* became impassable on foot.

Much as Kenneth Bradley loved the Luangwa, he reckoned that in the rainy season it was a 'green hell'.[10]

Previously Norman's hunting expeditions had been weekend excursions, involving two or three nights in the bush. As an elephant control officer and later as a game warden he had to spend weeks on end walking, working, and living in the bush. The Northern Rhodesia government equipped him with a substantial tent, a camp bed, and a variety of other items of safari equipment. These included a purpose designed chest in which food, table ware and kitchen gear could be packed: this was officially designated a deed box but universally known as a 'scoff box'. They also expected him to acquire a motor vehicle in which to travel to and from his base. In the height of the wet season this vehicle would have been of limited use. He provided his own rifles and ammunition. Finally, the government provided a budget of £108 per annum for hiring porters.

Porters were absolutely vital to Norman. On them his comfort and even his health depended. On *ulendo* the porters carried Norman's gear from one camp to the next. This frequently involved fording rivers. A set procedure for doing this was quickly established. The tallest porter had the honour of checking the depth and if he could cross without being washed away, albeit with his head submerged, then the others would follow. Norman was frequently washed downstream on these occasions and thought that this was because he did not carry any load whilst the porters' feet were more firmly planted because of the weight on their heads. Of particular concern were three vital loads – the tea, the sugar, and the ammunition. These were floated across in Norman's tin bath. Once a camp was established, it might remain in place for several days. Whilst Norman was out hunting, the cook and the porters would not be idle. One of their main tasks was to ensure that a fire was kept burning almost all of the time and that suitable firewood was available. On saturated ground and with heavy rain falling every afternoon this was no easy matter. Water for tea and for Norman's bath was heated on the cook's fire, in addition to food being prepared. Equally important was the campfire, sited to heat the tent during the night without filling it with smoke. Norman could sit close to this in the evenings if mosquitoes bothered him. During the day it was used to dry out bedding and clothes. It is not a coincidence that when Norman published a book about the trees of the Luangwa Valley in 1973, he included comments on those trees that provide particularly satisfactory firewood. He observed that mopane wood was the best because single logs could be kept burning all night. If the tent and bedding were not reasonably dry on mornings when camp was broken, then they would have to be packed wet. This added considerably to the weight that the porters had to carry and meant a miserably uncomfortable night ahead for Norman.

Norman had very good relations with his staff. There are several reasons for this. Firstly, he brought with him from the Secretariat in Zomba the knack of listening whilst others talked. He believed that if he spoke frequently then the porters and other staff would hesitate to express themselves. By staying quiet he got to know his companions as individual human beings and indeed he came to like them. Secondly, he fulfilled his duties as a *bwana wa nyama*. When dangerous animals had to be stalked, Norman took with him a tracker, a gun-bearer and maybe a porter too. Once he was close to his intended prey these companions were given time to climb up into trees for safety before he began the final stages of the hunt. In effect, Norman took as much as possible of the risk onto his own shoulders. Last, but not least, Norman provided his staff with ample - sometimes a superabundance of - food. Each elephant shot yielded several tons of meat and he was averaging more than one animal per day until December. So, the porters were consuming more protein than King George the Sixth in Buckingham Palace. For men who were accustomed to seasonal food shortages punctuated by occasional famines, an adequate supply of food was not something to be taken for granted.

The actual business of carrying out an elephant hunt is best described in Norman's own words:

In those days it seemed to me that hunting elephants was the most exhilarating pursuit in the world. One had to be in the pink of condition to stand the pace, travelling from sun-up to sun-down for weeks on end under the most arduous conditions. To catch up with the typical garden raider you must be prepared to journey over swampy ground, through impenetrable thickets and tall grass where the visibility is no more than an arm's length. Early in the morning the nine foot high elephant grass is saturated with dew and you become wetter and colder as the journey proceeds until the sun is high enough to dry you out. Then the humidity becomes stifling and bayonet-like grass seeds work their way through your clothing until you think you have reached the ultimate in discomfort: but not at all, for you have yet to meet the buffalo bean, an instrument of torture devised by the devil himself.[11]

On these occasions Norman was accompanied by an expert local tracker. As the weeks passed, he too became an expert in following and deciphering spoor (animal tracks) even when the tracks of several groups of elephants were intermingled.

Whilst Norman developed his expertise in bush craft and hunting, he remained a civil servant. His wife recalled that it was his habit to spend evenings busily working on official files, forms, and reports. She wrote:

... game rangers are civil servants, and in their office duties they display all the caution and pedantry usually associated with these meticulous people, but in most other respects they are very different.[12]

Early in September 1939, Norman parked his vehicle at the boma in Lundazi and set out to patrol in Chief Kambwiri's part of the Luangwa Valley. Two weeks later a district messenger brought him the news that Britain had declared war on Nazi Germany. Norman assumed that he would be needed immediately for service in the King's African Rifles, so he set off to walk to Lundazi. Over a period of 30 hours, he walked non-stop, covering about 100 miles. This epic journey ended in anticlimax. He was told that he would receive call-up papers once the army was ready to commission him. The British armed forces were in the process of expanding from less than a million men to over 5 million and this massive growth would require a huge effort of planning and logistics. So, Norman returned to his recently started career as a game ranger.

Crop Protection: Northern Province

Before Christmas 1939, Norman was transferred from the Eastern Province to the Northern Province. He had to make his way from Fort Jameson to Kasama. As the rainy season had started, it would have been normal for Norman, as a civil servant, to make this journey by lorry. Lorries went back and forth between Fort Jameson and Lusaka regularly, but travel was slow because the heavy rains made the road conditions difficult. Once in Lusaka he would have to wait until a lorry with sufficient space was available to transport him and his considerable accumulation of safari equipment to Kasama.

Norman decided to walk to Kasama. This involved climbing the Muchinga escarpment, the western wall of the Luangwa Valley. Norman was excited by the prospect of experiencing the escarpment at close quarters: hitherto he had only seen it as a purple bar on the horizon. It is a tribute to his standing that he had no difficulty in recruiting the 22 porters needed for this exacting journey. Of course, on a *ulendo* like this each camp would remain in place for a single night. So, it was guaranteed that his bedding and tent would become progressively wetter and wetter over time. Eventually there was mildew growing on his blankets. When Norman reported for duty in Kasama the provincial commissioner made it plain that he regarded Norman's decision to walk up the escarpment as evidence of a serious lack of judgement, verging on insanity. By the time he had reached Mpika, ten days after setting off from the Luangwa River, even Norman was willing to take shelter in a rest house. At Mpika Norman discharged his original crew of porters and engaged a new, mainly Bemba speaking, group. He also visited the grave of Charlie Ross, his predecessor as crop protection officer.

In the Northern Province, Norman took full advantage of the opportunity to see as much as possible of the country. Over a period of six months, he walked over a thousand miles and moved between the densely forested high plateau and the low-lying marshes and rivers. On the Luapula River Norman faced the greatest natural barrier to effective crop protection that he was ever to encounter. Here the *mateshi* thickets grew right to the water's edge. Local people created small vegetable gardens by laboriously cutting down and rooting out the vegetation. These gardens were regularly raided by elephants which simply shouldered the *mateshi* bush aside.

When Norman tried to follow, he found it quite impossible. Weeks of toil resulted in just three elephants shot; this was wholly inadequate to bring about significant behavioural change in the remaining elephants. He even had to shoot antelopes to feed his porters.

Whilst he was based in the Northern Province, Norman was allocated a bungalow at the remote out–station of Luwingu. Here he made the acquaintance of Arthur Benson, the district commissioner. Benson and his wife were particularly hospitable and when Norman arrived, having undertaken his epic journey from Fort Jameson via Mpika and Kasama, they persuaded him to take a week to rest and get all his gear clean and dry. Later, as Sir Arthur, Benson was to become governor of Northern Rhodesia.

The King's African Rifles

On 13 July 1940 Norman was called up and commissioned as a lieutenant in the King's African Rifles. His pay as an officer was £456 per annum plus a £20 allowance for kit. This was slightly higher than his £400 pay as a game ranger. His colleagues had taken care to ensure that he accrued continuous service for pension purposes when he moved from Nyasaland to Northern Rhodesia. His war service would count for superannuation too – if he lived long enough to draw a pension. In November 1940 he and Barbara Lennon were married. After a honeymoon at Lake Nyasa (Malawi) devoted largely to shooting crocodiles, the newly-weds settled down at an army training camp close to the border with Portuguese East Africa (Mozambique). Here Norman was a company commander responsible for about 120 African soldiers. More will be said about Barbara and their family life below.

The global situation in July 1940 was very different from that of September 1939. France had been defeated and, thinking that easy pickings were now available, the Italian dictator Mussolini had declared war on Britain. This created a threatening situation in Africa. The Italians had colonies in the three adjacent territories of Abyssinia (now Ethiopia), Eritrea and Somaliland and in Libya. In Abyssinia and the neighbouring countries, the Italians had a quarter of a million troops plus some local irregulars. They had excellent artillery, significant naval forces in the Red Sea and sufficient air forces (including fast bomber aircraft) to give them air superiority. There was real anxiety about a possible Italian invasion of Kenya. After some small, localised attacks, the Italians adopted a defensive strategy. In due course approximately 80,000 Commonwealth troops assembled in the bleak and parched Northern Frontier Province of Kenya to launch an offensive. As they took up their positions in a landscape of black pumice stone, they could see the mountains occupied by Italian troops who thus had the advantage of high ground. Of the total force, over 30,000 were from South Africa and Southern Rhodesia (Zimbabwe) where black Africans were not permitted to undertake combat duties. A further 42,000 soldiers on the British side served in colonial regiments that were overwhelmingly made up of black Africans. Once a separate force had assembled in the Sudan, simultaneous invasions were mounted from both north and south. The battalions of the King's African Rifles that were already in Kenya acquitted themselves well in this fighting.

Norman's first task in the army was to train African recruits. The King's African Rifles had been in existence for decades and had plenty of seasoned and reliable African non-commissioned officers (corporals, sergeants, etc) who would have constituted the backbone of the training programme. Norman's NCOs were led by Sergeant Liasala who was an expert tracker. Norman would have had to draw on his own experience in the Nyasaland Volunteers to train recruits in drill – the intensive training in formation marching and stylised weapons handling that formed the core of initial training throughout the army. Once the recruits had mastered parade ground soldiering, they were trained in the use of their weapons and introduced to military field craft – the art of making use of terrain to minimise risk and maximise opportunity. Norman's experience as a game ranger equipped him well for this role. Most of 1941 was devoted to training his company for operations in Abyssinia. Twice Norman was called on to hunt lions during 1941. On the first occasion the objective was to protect livestock. On the second, he had to deal with two man-eaters that had killed eleven people in just two weeks around Chief Namwera's village.

At the end of 1941, Norman's unit was posted to Abyssinia. Before he left a decision had to be made regarding which of the recently married couple's domestic servants should accompany him as a batman (officer's orderly and servant). The choice lay between Aliki and Mateyu (of whom more will be said below). On the grounds that Mateyu was married with small children it was agreed that Aliki who was unmarried should accompany Norman. The unfortunate Aliki never came back. He was murdered by Abyssinian bandits much to the distress of his elderly parents.

By the time that Norman and his comrades reached Abyssinia the campaign was effectively over. The surrender of the Italian forces at the fortress of Gondar in November 1941 marked the end of large-scale hostilities. Nonetheless, there was plenty for the Commonwealth troops to do. Resistance by small groups of Italian soldiers continued. In August 1942, the main ammunition dump in Addis Ababa was sabotaged by Italian guerrillas. Even more serious was the threat from irregular Abyssinian forces and outright bandits, these represented a threat to Italian civilians, Italian prisoners of war and to the infrastructure of the country. Bridges, power stations, the main railway line and telephone communications all needed to be guarded against theft and wanton destruction whilst the Ethiopian king's interim administration was establishing itself. The significance of this task can be readily appreciated if the experience of Iraq and Afghanistan in the wake of twenty-first century American-led invasions is used as a yardstick of comparison. Whilst in Addis Ababa, Norman discovered the identity of Bwana Chiduli whom he had chased after in the Luangwa Valley. Chiduli turned out to be Captain Peter Hankin who was serving with the Royal Artillery. The two became good friends and subsequently they became business partners in the 1960s.

The soldiers of the King's African Rifles had shown courage and determination when engaged in ground fighting. However, they had demonstrated a tendency to panic when subjected to air attack. As a result, the British high command was reluctant to deploy them in North Africa where they would have been exposed to Italian and German air raids. They were, however, regarded as being suitable to fight in the Far East against the Japanese.

Towards the end of 1942 Norman was sent to the Tactical School at Gilgil in Kenya to undergo training for jungle warfare. He possessed many of the attributes that the British army looked for in its officers. He possessed evident courage and considerable physical strength. He spoke the language of the soldiers under his command and found it easy to empathise with and lead them. He was a marksman and had well-developed field craft skills. But in 1943 Norman was demobilised and sent back to Northern Rhodesia to resume civilian life. It is tempting to seek an explanation in terms of his own conduct, but the real reason had little to do with Norman as an individual. The explanation can be expressed in one word – tea.

Tea was vital to the British army both on active service and in rear bases. In Victorian times Rudyard Kipling had remarked that 'when it comes to slaughter, you'll do your work on water'[13] but by the 1940s that had changed. British generals and the British government believed that tea was refreshing and calming and when taken with generous quantities of sugar or condensed milk provided an energy boost. General Wavell observed that Australian soldiers, of whom he had a high opinion, drank even more tea than their British counterparts. Nyasaland and Kenya were both major tea-producing areas. Demand for their products had risen between 1939 and 1943 whilst output had declined. It was recognised that a major factor in the fall in production was the absence on military service of many farmers and plantation managers. So, a decision was made to discharge a substantial number of locally recruited officers from the King's African Rifles and to replace them with young men from the United Kingdom. Norman's peacetime job was crop protection, so it was natural that he should be discharged as part of the exercise.

In fact, many of the soldiers of the King's African Rifles never left Africa. They played a major role in maintaining order in Abyssinia until 1943. They also guarded Italian prisoners of war who were moved to Kenya and employed on large road construction projects. In addition, they provided guard forces for the East African ports and for installations that might have been vulnerable to sabotage by the Japanese. Had Norman remained in the army he would probably have spent his time in enforced idleness and boredom.

Chapter 4

Marriage and Family Life

Late in 1940 Norman married Barbara Lennon. In some respects, their marriage was a classic wartime romance. He was handsome and looked particularly dashing in the dress uniform of the King's African Rifles, including a black ostrich plume in his Australian-style slouch hat. Norman had even grown an infantry officer's neatly trimmed moustache. Barbara was an attractive and articulate young woman. She also had a rebellious streak but, as the daughter and granddaughter of soldiers, she was no less susceptible to the allure of a uniform than other women.

Barbara had been born in Dagshai in Iraq where her father James R. Lennon was serving in the British army. Lennon had been born in India and his father had sent him to the Duke of York's School in Chelsea - a school for the sons of soldiers. His formal education had ended at an early age when he, too, had joined the army. Lennon had been on active service with the army in France and then Iraq between 1914 and 1920. He wanted his children to have the opportunities that education can bring and that he had not had. So, when he left the armed forces in 1931, he joined the colonial service. A major attraction of the colonial service was that it provided financial assistance towards officers' children's educational costs. Lennon was fortunate that he was posted to the prison service in Nyasaland where crime levels were low and a humane approach was taken.

In Zomba, Lennon was in charge of the central prison from 1931 until 1939. This prison served a large part of the country and held most of those serving long sentences for serious crimes. The Superintendent of Prisons, Lennon's boss, was Jack Archer. Archer, like Lennon, had been a non-commissioned officer in the British army, and had served in South Africa and Somaliland, rising to the rank of regimental sergeant major. He was taken prisoner in one of the opening battles of the First World War. Like all prisoners of war or POWs held in Germany, Archer endured hunger. In winter POWs were also acutely cold, as little fuel was provided for their use. As the highest-ranking NCO in the camp, Archer was singled out for a sustained campaign of intimidation by the camp guards. This included the threat of beatings, simulated assaults and a prolonged barrage of verbal abuse. This experience gave Archer an insight into the vulnerability of prison inmates and he brought to the role of superintendent a sincere desire to treat them as human beings. Together, Archer and Lennon carried out the abolition of chain gang labour, monitored warders with a view to eliminating abusive behaviour, ensured that adequate food was provided, and that decent standards of hygiene were maintained. Nonetheless, hangings had to be carried out in accordance with the law. Lennon invariably attended these although he found them profoundly depressing. Archer and Lennon were both active members of the Nyasaland Volunteers and Norman probably first met his future father-in-law through this territorial unit. Lennon was promoted to Deputy Superintendent of Prisons and Asylums in 1939 and succeeded Archer as Superintendent in 1945.

In 1931, as the Lennon family prepared to leave the UK for Nyasaland, arrangements were made for Barbara to attend a girls' boarding school in Britain. Her father left for Zomba expecting that he would not see his daughter for several years. He was furious when he discovered that Barbara had persuaded her mother to change these plans, which Barbara did by pleading that she would be miserable in a boarding school. Lennon determined to provide his daughter with a demanding regime of home schooling. As part of this she had to play hockey at the Gymkhana Club on Saturdays. Her father was the referee and made sure that she felt the pressure that came with being the youngest and smallest member of the team. Lennon was an intelligent and widely-read man. Nonetheless, the course of study he developed for his daughter was unconventional and reflected his own interests. So Barbara read lots of Kipling but no Shakespeare, learnt an extraordinary amount about the history of the British army but nothing about British prime ministers, and devoted a good deal of time to ornithology but little to mathematics. Lennon had set up bird hides at several locations around Zomba and it is clear that Barbara enjoyed spending time with him on birdwatching outings as he was relaxed and jovial on these occasions. He had reptile pits in his garden and was sufficiently scientific in his study of reptiles to have his collection of specimens accepted by the British Museum. Whilst in Zomba, Barbara passed through puberty. She had the advantage that her mother, rather than a school matron, had the task of guiding and advising her during this important transition.

Barbara later recalled that for much of the year, whilst the family was in Zomba, they lived in a government house within sight of the prison gates. Her fondest memories, however, were of the time that the family spent on Zomba Mountain. Each year in the hot weather, when temperatures reached a point that made it difficult to sleep at night, the Lennon family rented a cottage on the plateau 2500 feet above the town. Life here was a source of delight, with pleasant sunshine, cool breezes, masses of butterflies flitting between the trees, picnics and swimming parties around the Mulunguzi stream.

At the age of 14 Barbara left Zomba to attend a conventional school in the UK. Her younger brother Steve was making the transition to senior school at the same time and their mother moved to the UK in order to be close to them. During her time at school, Barbara exchanged letters in Cinyanja with Mateyu, the most senior member of her father's staff. At the outbreak of the Second World War Mrs Lennon and her children were still in the UK, living in the Channel Islands close to the coast of France. James Lennon was concerned about the safety of his family. He apparently had serious doubts about the fighting qualities of the French army. So early in 1940 James asked that Barbara, who had completed her schooling, should join him in Nyasaland and take on the role of housekeeper. The rest of the family were to follow once her brother had completed his schooling. The cost of Barbara's travel was met by the Nyasaland government.

Barbara was shocked by the state of affairs in her father's household. He exercised little supervision over his servants and, despite Mateyu's presence, there was wholesale theft from the stores. Tea and sugar were particularly subject to pilfering because they were easily traded. Also, the servants had developed the habit of mixing paraffin with the floor polish in order to get a brilliant shine: this created a very real fire risk. All of this was combined with what she regarded as chronic idleness. Although she was not yet 20 years old, Barbara asserted her authority and achieved significant economies in household expenditure.

During this period Barbara acted as hostess for her father. Dinner parties for officers of the colonial service and their wives had to be planned and catered for. These events made her aware of the seemingly absurd and petty rules that governed who must sit where and who must be accorded precedence. It now became clear to her that her father, to whom she had become close and for whom she had a high regard, occupied a lowly position in the colonial hierarchy. Primarily this was because his job ranked below many others. In addition, the fact that he had served in the army but had not been an officer counted against him. This may have rankled more with her than it did with him.

Once the whole Lennon family was reunited in Zomba in mid-1940, Barbara handed over responsibility for domestic management to her mother and took a job in the civil service. She was rapidly promoted to become head of the open registry in the Secretariat. This was the same building that Norman had worked in but, whereas he had been in charge of the confidential registry that was located upstairs and was only accessible to British staff, she was downstairs where record-keeping was largely in the hands of African staff. She was not impressed and wrote:

> '[Jasper] enters the post in the register and files it' Des [Rochester, her predecessor as head of registry] said to me as we sat down. 'But we have to check every darn thing he does because he always manages to make mistakes. He'll put a letter about the new native hospital in the Tobacco in the Northern Province file.'
>
> [On another day] 'Where's Jasper?' I asked.
>
> 'Oh, he hasn't come in. He often doesn't. We shan't miss him. It'll take us half an hour to do his work.' ... Des was right about Jasper's work and we polished it off in less than an hour. No wonder the native clerks always look as if they're doing nothing, I thought. They are.
>
> ... I asked Des 'Why don't we give them more to do?'
>
> 'Because they're ruddy well not capable, that's why,' said Des...[14]

This view, however, was not universally held within the colonial service. At a meeting of district commissioners in 1935, the subject of delegation of responsibility to native staff was discussed and

> ... it was agreed ... it was necessary to weed out inefficient members of the higher grades ... [and that] ... this country loses the services of natives with real ability since they can find much better-paid employment abroad ....[15]

As was normal at that time, Barbara resigned this job on her marriage. After a honeymoon at the Lake, during which Norman shot crocodiles in order to examine their stomach contents, the newly-weds settled at an army training camp near the Portuguese East African border where she was the only European woman. Here Norman taught her to fire a rifle. When he left for Abyssinia, she returned to Zomba where she worked as a confidential cypher clerk. In 1942 when Norman went to the Tactical School at Gilgil in Kenya, Barbara left her job and made a lengthy and roundabout journey to be near him. She lived amongst farmers' wives, most of whom had been left to manage the farms whilst their husbands served in the armed forces, mainly the KARs. Barbara found this an alarming experience as the attitude of the farm workers seemed to her to be truculent at best and sometimes openly hostile.

Instead of being sent to fight in Burma, Norman was sent back to Zomba, as has been explained in the previous chapter. At this point he could have made a major career change in order that his pregnant wife could have a settled life. A number of new civil service jobs had been created, mainly as supplies officers and labour officers. Norman would have had little difficulty in securing one of these jobs. The colonial authorities needed these officers because they had introduced price controls and rationing of petrol and clothing. They were seeking also to expand the output of products useful in the war effort. Norman could have chosen to work in Lusaka or Blantyre where his unborn child would have had the chance of an uninterrupted primary education and Barbara would have had company. It is doubtful though, that he gave this serious consideration until many years later: the dedication in his book *The White Impala* reads 'To Judy, Pamela and Adrian whose well-being I have neglected in my pursuit of adventure in out-of-the-way places'. In 1943, the wilderness had him spellbound. On demobilisation Norman received an ex-serviceman's gratuity. It is symbolic that he spent this on buying a sturdy high-clearance Dodge vanette that would enable him to go about his work. There was a shortage of government vehicles at the time because the war effort took priority. The vehicle, however, turned out to be a financial millstone. Each month the running costs exceeded the allowances and expenses provided by the government by about £20 – approximately one third of Norman's salary. Barbara summarised their life together as follows:

> 'In twelve years we had twenty-seven house moves, seven station transfers, one overseas leave and three babies.'[16]

Norman spent forty weeks of each year in the bush discharging his duties as a game ranger. As they had perennial financial problems, he spent a large part of his local leave on hunting expeditions. By shooting elephants and selling the tusks he supplemented their income considerably. These prolonged absences created personal tensions between Norman and Barbara, not least because they deprived her of his support in child care. Emily Bradley, wife of Kenneth Bradley who had been DC in Fort Jameson for much of the 1920s and 1930s, wrote on the basis of her experiences that colonial officers were usually much better fathers than their counterparts at home:

> I remember also the time both my sons had whooping-cough … Father was on duty until twelve, and I got five or six hours of undisturbed rest. After midnight it was his turn to sleep and mine to … hold the terrified sufferer while he fought, pacify the other who had been disturbed by the noise … mop up and try to sleep again.[17]

Norman's long absences also contributed to the practical difficulties of Barbara's life as only Norman was permitted to report problems with their house and furniture to the Public Works Department. If the roof leaked or the mosquito netting was torn, Barbara might wait months for the problem to be addressed. This was further compounded by Norman's reluctance to make a fuss about accommodation. If he was told that the oldest and most dilapidated bungalow on a station was the only one available then he was not inclined to argue; his career as a game ranger was too precious to him. In effect, Norman accepted the outward signs of low status just as his father-in-law had done.

The repeated house moves were particularly dismal in their effects. Several of these transient 'homes' were leave houses which the Carrs occupied only for as long as the usual occupants were in the UK on holiday. This meant that Barbara had to employ the servants who came with the house and dismiss her previous ones. The primary loyalty of leave-house staff was to their absent employer. In at least one instance, the servants held keys for rooms that they had been instructed not to allow the Carrs to use. In these were stored the absent family's best furniture and household equipment. Yet the Carrs had to pay rent for the house and pay the servants' wages. Barbara took comfort from the presence of Mateyu with whom she had corresponded whilst at school. On her wedding, Barbara's parents had asked Mateyu to take employment with her. He had been the most reliable and trustworthy member of the Lennons' household. He was a member of the warrior Ngoni tribe but also a devout Roman Catholic. Barbara wrote of him:

> In those lonely days in the bush Mateyu was my best friend … [and] shared with me the joys and anxieties of my young motherhood …. I don't know what I would have done without Mateyu in those long, lonely years. He had been my father's batman and my mother's major-domo for fifteen years before they asked him to work for me. He was … always a tender and solicitous guardian to me and the children.[18]

Mateyu may also have been the source of some of the difficulties that Barbara experienced with her other servants. As an Ngoni he was an outsider in many of their postings and it is likely that he regarded his colleagues with contempt both on account of their own shortcomings and their perceived ethnic inferiority. Be that as it may, he remained loyal to the family and eventually served Norman's mother, Emily Carr, when she moved to Lusaka in the 1960s.

Emily Bradley wrote a book giving advice to women who married colonial civil servants. In this she stressed the importance of finding worthwhile activities and interests whilst simultaneously accepting the limitations inherent in being a woman in a man's world. She listed as possible occupations: making clothes, gardening, social and voluntary work, craft skills, study of local languages, whist, reading, writing, and developing the skills of the domestic staff (particularly the cook). Barbara did make clothes, particularly for her daughters but did not derive any satisfaction from doing so, saying the garments made them look like orphans. She rarely had the good fortune to take over a house that already possessed a good garden. When she did attempt to grow her own vegetables this was a disaster. Ironically, given that Norman's job involved crop protection, her vegetables were destroyed by wild animals. Barbara despised 'good works' and was apt to cause offence to those who devoted time and energy to child welfare clinics, Girl Guides, and other activities for the benefit of African women and children. This may have contributed to her sense of isolation. She did not take an interest in handicrafts, nor did she expand her knowledge of African languages beyond the Cinyanja that she had learnt in childhood. In fact she despaired at the prospect of losing her grasp of English through lack of use: 'sometimes for months on end I talked nothing but nursery language to the children, Cinyanja to the natives and a garbled sort of English to myself.'[19] Barbara was later to write two books but during her marriage to Norman her output was limited to occasional articles for newspapers. Nor did she get any joy from developing the skills of her domestic staff. There was little that she could teach Mateyu and she quickly fell into the habit of regarding the rest of her staff as a lost cause.

One puzzle is why Barbara did not take up the opportunities for bird watching that her itinerant life provided. She had enjoyed ornithological study with her father and to have continued that would have given her a shared interest with Norman who confessed that his knowledge of birds was not equal to his knowledge of mammals, trees and habitat. In Tanganyika [Tanzania] Cicely Ruggles-Brise had provided an example. She took up bird watching whilst acting as housekeeper to her brother, the DC in Morogoro. She had published the first field guide to the birds of Dar es Salaam and become a Fellow of the Royal Zoological Society.

Norman's first posting following war service was to Lusaka. Then he was transferred to Kasempa, where he remained for about one year. During this period Barbara returned to her parents' home in Zomba for the birth of her daughters Judy in 1943 and Pam in 1945. It is evident that she regarded the people of Zomba, both African and European, as being nicer and better company than their counterparts in Northern Rhodesia. In 1945 Norman got his dream-come-true and was posted to the Luangwa Valley. The Carrs made their home in Fort Jameson. Here Barbara was able to engage a hard-working and reliable 18-year-old, the mixed-race daughter of a provincial commissioner and an African woman, to look after her children whilst she worked. Barbara had two part-time jobs, one as a newspaper reporter and the other as an office clerk for the African Lakes Company. This was probably her best chance for happiness. Fort Jameson had a substantial European population and a good-sized club. Yet even here she felt that work was the only thing that prevented her from stagnating. She made no effort to become part of a whist-playing set or otherwise to engage with her peers. Things were to get a good deal worse when future postings took the Carrs to very remote places. In the classic 1940s film *In which we Serve* a naval officer's wife is offered advice about her rival – his ship – to the effect that she should not fight against his affection for, and attachment to, his ship because naval wives who do that that end up feeling hurt.

Emily Bradley offered similar advice in relation to the colonial service. All the indicators suggest that within a few years of their marriage Barbara had made up her mind to reject such ideas. She categorised game rangers as:

> 'Bachelors suffering from arrested development'
> 'Married men with fierce wives who refused hardship postings'
> 'Married men who behaved as if they were not'[20]

There is little doubt that she saw Norman as falling in the last category. She got into the habit of storing up complaints and demands in preparation for Norman's homecoming. It is telling that Norman devoted most of his local leave to elephant hunting, ostensibly in order to augment their income. Under the game laws the maximum number of elephants that a hunter could shoot was four. Norman was capable of shooting that number in two days but commonly absented himself for two weeks on these freelance safaris. Even if we make allowances on the basis that he would have let go animals with tusks below fifty pounds in weight, and waited for more lucrative targets, it is pretty clear that he did not need to spend a fortnight in the bush to 'bag' four elephants. It is reasonable to draw the conclusion that as early as 1945 his relationship with Barbara had reached the point where he preferred to spend time in the bush rather than in her company. Almost certainly Barbara had begun to acquire a reputation as what was known in the colonial service slang as 'a purple cow' – a woman who was constantly grumbling, all too evidently uninterested in other women's children and domestic activities, and suspected of sneering at their voluntary work for the natives.

Chapter 5

The Luangwa Valley and the Birth of Community-based Wildlife Conservation

Kasempa

After demobilisation, Norman's first posting was to Lusaka. Then he was transferred to Kasempa, a small settlement in which the headquarters of the North Western Province was located. Here Norman undertook a familiar round of arduous anti-poaching and crop protection patrols. He also sought a workable resolution of the challenge posed to European notions of conservation by the Ila people and their hunting traditions. The Ila people were a cattle-keeping ethnic group who lived in an extensive area to the south of Kasempa in the direction of the Kafue River. They had long-established customs that involved an annual buffalo hunt and occasional lechwe hunts, known as *chila* on the fringes of the Kafue Flats. As an experienced hunter himself, Norman was inclined to regard the annual buffalo hunt as a display of manly courage that served to keep alive traditional virtues and skills.

The buffalo hunt took place late in the dry season on the east bank of the Kafue where seasonal drought caused the animals to congregate in search of drinking water. On the night before the hunt, a traditional 'dance of courage' was performed at which both women and alcoholic drinks were prohibited. In the morning a prayer was said to animist spirits. Then fire was used to drive the animals into tightly packed groups. Barbara Carr was present at one hunt and has left a vivid account of it:

> The animals wheeled in a cloud of ash and thundered towards
> the lagoon. When they were about twenty yards from the water

a dozen or so hunters ... suddenly jumped up and hurled their spears. Some buffalo stopped dead in their tracks ... while others ran on. ... The bellows of the crazed beasts, the thudding of their hoofs as they stampeded in all directions, and the blood curdling yells of the natives made me block my ears. So much, I thought bitterly, for the skill and bravery of the Ba Ila tribesmen. They were not brave; they were simply wild ...[21]

She added:

Norman thought this was a fine old custom and one that helped to keep ancient African tradition alive. (Whatever for?) I failed to see how the natives could continue to indulge in this barbaric practice and at the same time imbibe even the rudiments of western culture.[22]

What Barbara seems to have overlooked is that this once-in-a-year event had resulted in the death of just 50 buffalo out of a herd of 2,000. Under the watchful eye of the game warden and his game guards the loss had been just 2.5 per cent. In the process, Norman had established a working relationship with key leaders of the Ila people which would later prove valuable when he was tasked with taking over the Kafue National Park. This forms the subject of a later chapter.

Barbara responded to the *chila*, the hunt for lechwe water antelopes, that she witnessed in much the same way as to the buffalo hunt, saying that it '... horrified and alarmed ...' her.[23] In support of her position Barbara quoted a publication by Dr Frank Fraser Darling in which he too condemned the practice of lechwe hunting. However, she neglected to mention that Darling had not actually attended a *chila* and relied entirely on particular members of staff at the Department of Game and Tsetse Control for information on the matter.

Department of Game and Tsetse Control

The creation of this department had been recommended in 1934 in a report by Captain Pitman, Game Warden of Uganda. The Northern Rhodesia government had declined to create a separate department straight away. Instead they appointed four crop protection officers who would work under the direction of provincial commissioners. This was the system in place when Norman became a crop protection officer in 1938. By the time he returned from military service, things had moved on.

In 1942 a fully-fledged Department of Game and Tsetse Control had been set up with T G C Vaughan-Jones as the Acting Director. Vaughan-Jones had studied at Oxford University and had been a district officer. In 1946 he was confirmed as Director of the Department of Game and Tsetse Control; in 1956 he moved on to become Commissioner for Rural Development. The Game Department was based in Chilanga, approximately 12 miles south of Lusaka because there was an acute shortage of office accommodation in the colonial capital in wartime. The department had an establishment of 12 senior (i.e. European) staff, although some of these posts were not filled. It may appear odd that such a department was created in the middle of the Second World War. Changes in the financial situation of the Northern Rhodesia government are relevant in this context. In 1934 public revenues were just starting to recover from the great depression, whereas by 1942 the copper mines were in full production and tax receipts had risen dramatically. As the annual report on Northern Rhodesia states: 'Annual Revenue rose from little over £1,500,000 in 1938 to £3,433,507 in 1945.'[24]

The official policy of the department, based on the Pitman Report, was that land in Northern Rhodesia should be divided into two distinct types. The first was intended for human occupation: here the department would protect crops and, where necessary, would exterminate wild animals in order to eradicate tsetse flies and thereby make cattle keeping possible. The second type consisted of animal sanctuaries in which no hunting or other economic activity would be permitted. Pitman had made it quite explicit that additional game reserves should be created and that their human inhabitants should be removed. The only intermediate position that was envisaged was where 'controlled areas' were created and licensed hunting permitted.

The organisational culture of the department was in essence one of command and control. It was not envisaged that African peoples would be engaged in any process of dialogue to find mutually acceptable outcomes. It was taken for granted that the conservation of wildlife was a good thing in itself and that the creation of sanctuaries required no justification. A command and control approach came naturally to many of the senior staff, not least after 1945 when a significant number of discharged military officers took up posts. To say this is not to demonise the people involved. Whilst in the armed forces, many had developed characteristics of courage and fortitude that would stand them in good stead when working as game wardens or in other roles. One was Paddy Dunn, the game ranger at Kabompo who had been awarded the Distinguished Service Cross for his service as an officer in the Royal Navy during the Battle of the Atlantic. Another was Major Eustace Poles, game warden at Mpika. Poles had commanded a guerrilla force that operated in a remote area of Burma, well removed from the main body of British troops. He had shown considerable resourcefulness and courage in attacking the Japanese and was awarded the Military Cross. He liked people to think that he had been a professional soldier before the war began and, to this end, cultivated a fierce and regimental attitude. In reality he had been a policeman in civilian life. Poles expressed the collective view of his colleagues when he wrote:

> Unfortunately it appears that the Provincial Administration officers control the policy of our department. They insist on the retention of the practice of game netting …. They allow practically every other native to …. own muzzle-loaders and encourage the African to purchase breech-loading shotguns. What can this lead to except the extermination of every living thing?[25]

This viewpoint was expressed forcefully to Sir Frank Fraser Darling, an academic from Edinburgh University, who was the Colonial Office's favoured adviser on ecology. Following visits to Northern Rhodesia in the 1950s, he faithfully articulated the standard perspective of the Department of Game and Tsetse Control:

> The game has been hunted out by Africans with muzzle-loading guns. Northern Rhodesia allows Africans to have these and the effect on game over large areas is disastrous. The African is incapable of conservation sense and the Administration here is exceptionally soft towards the African …. European hunting is no serious factor now.[26]

Darling added

> [Chief] Nabwalia is a contant thorn in the Game Department's side, and …. the Provincial Commissioner will use Nabwalia to spike the Game Department's guns. I have learned something of the scandalous way in which the Labour Government pushed promising young Socialists into the Colonial Service and their conduct of affairs here is appalling.[27] (p.36)

Norman Carr did not naturally 'fit' in this department. With his subordinates he had a good relationship which was based on a degree of understanding and mutual respect. He was the boss, certainly, but he could achieve results without resort to kicking or belittling his porters and game guards.

Carr's position within his department was further complicated because he had a much better insight into the problems and challenges facing the district commissioners than most of his colleagues. In addition, Norman empathised with their desire to help African people. Although the British Colonial Service has come in for much criticism since the 1960s, it remains the case that most district commissioners sincerely believed that their job was to protect African people and to help them achieve economic development. For example, the DC for Mkipa wrote in 1953: 'The Game Department must ... be judged notoriously heedless of the rights of person and property where it is considered these conflict in any way with the consideration of the fauna'.[28] On the basis of his work in the Secretariat in Zomba, where maintaining the filing system had given him a grand overview of government, Norman understood that the Provincial Administration were constrained by a variety of considerations. Whatever they did must comply with the law. It must be feasible within tight budgetary limitations. Above all, it must comply with the stated policy of the British government and Parliament – that the interests of native African peoples were paramount. Whilst serving as a crop protection officer, Carr had developed a strong admiration for the district commissioners as men. One man that he particularly liked was Arthur Benson, the DC at Luwingu in the Northern Province. They became acquainted in the late 1930s. Benson returned to Northern Rhodesia, as Governor Sir Arthur Benson, after a varied career spent in Uganda, Nigeria and the Colonial Office in London.

If Norman Carr had left the army in 1945 it is likely that he would have found it difficult to be fully accepted by his colleagues. Fortunately, he joined just a few months after Vaughan-Jones had started the organisation from scratch. Norman's standing and experience as a founder member of staff was to his advantage. So too was the fact that he spent so much of his time in the bush. Once he was away from the provincial headquarters, the only way in which his director could communicate with him was by dispatching a district messenger with a written communication: that was a last resort. So long as Norman compiled his field reports on time and kept his accounts to the satisfaction of the auditors, he was able to lead a largely autonomous existence.

The Luangwa Valley and the Development of a Conservationist

In the years following Norman's return from military service, his thinking about wildlife and conservation developed dramatically. Instead of being interested in large animals only, he had begun to notice '… the ecology of my environment.'[29] Trees, soil and vegetation began to interest him. So did small birds. It would appear that he had started to read widely on aspects of ecology that previously held no interest for him. Norman began to regret that he had failed to take the opportunity to discuss these matters with Colin Trapnell who had been the Northern Rhodesia Government ecologist in the 1930s.[30] Carr knew that Trapnell had carried out experiments concerning the management of bush fires. Trapnell's conclusion was that where habitats were to be managed for the benefit of wildlife then the traditional practice of starting fires at the end of the dry season was harmful. 'Hot burning' in October could do lasting damage to shrubs and trees and was often devastating for ground-nesting birds. Trapnell advocated 'cool burning' in May instead as this did less damage and prevented 'hot burning' by consuming much of the fuel. Trapnell had been a contemporary of both Sir Arthur Benson and T G C Vaughan-Jones at Oxford University. Colin Trapnell left Northern Rhodesia to become the officer in charge of ecological training in a research organisation in East Africa.

At this time, Carr began to realise that both land and wildlife were resources and that conservation projects must deliver benefits for human beings if they were to be sustainable in the long-term. As a result, he became aware of the inadequacies of the 'sanctuary' approach where large areas were set aside and all human activity prohibited. Both licensed hunting and game viewing had the potential to contribute to wildlife conservation by generating revenue. Norman articulated this view in his book, *The White Impala:*

> The days are past, especially in Africa, when large tracts of undeveloped land can be set aside as game sanctuaries purely for sentimental or aesthetic reasons. In view of the human population explosion …. it has become imperative that the natural resources

should be fully harnessed and developed; otherwise the land will be entirely usurped for purposes which could be inimical to the animals.[31]

The development of Norman's thinking was probably shaped in significant ways during his overseas leave in 1953. The whole family went to Britain and their visit was timed to coincide with the coronation of Queen Elizabeth the Second. Whilst they were in London he attended a short and intensive course in Zoology at the University of London. He participated also in a new course devised by the Zoological Society of London specifically at the request of the Colonial Office and tailored especially for staff with wildlife conservation responsibilities. The Zoological Society of London annual report for the year described it thus: 'The course gave instruction on systematics, physiology and ecology of animals, with particular reference to the animals of Africa.'[32]

Chief Nsefu's Game Reserve – a Simplified Version

In 1950 Chief Nsefu, in collaboration with Norman Carr, created the first community-based animal conservation and viewing area. Norman's published account of this development is worth quoting at length

> As a game ranger, I had a free hand from my head of department ... There were, of course, inhibiting factors, one of which was the conservative policy of the colonial regime .... Normally under these rules no restrictive legislation would be considered which affected ... the residents in Trust Land (the greater part of all rural areas) without consultation and acceptance by the people themselves. Therefore any scheme aimed at creating a non-hunting area ... was virtually impossible, unless one could persuade the chief that it was to his advantage.
> Paramount Chief Nsefu, who ruled over the Akunda people, was ... a kindly, white haired old man with a ready smile. He was a personal friend ... I spoke to him about the possibility of converting this camp [Chipera] into a place where visitors could come and view game. He was not at first enthusiastic, for he had always lived alongside wild animals and could not imagine anyone coming all that way just to see them. ... He still could not understand why anyone would leave those wonderful brick houses with all their magic gadgets just to come and stay in the bush. However, the prospect of obtaining some financial reward ... was enough to enlist his co-operation.

> I could find nothing in General Orders which forbade me from … using my porters to build this new game camp for the chief. A track for motors had to be made into the camp so I recruited a further gang who were only too pleased to be paid for their labour in buffalo meat. I managed to borrow some basic furniture … and scrounged round for the … pieces of equipment necessary to get the camp started. And this is how the first game viewing camp in Northern Rhodesia was opened to the public in July 1950. The ten shillings entrance fee charged to visitors went directly to the chief.
>
> After the first year Chief Nsefu needed little encouragement to apply officially for a game reserve to be declared around his camp in order to protect his interests. … Nsefu Game Reserve of approximately eighty-three square miles was officially proclaimed the following year.[33]

This account has all the virtues of Norman's writing. It is concise, lucid and straightforward. However, a fuller version of the creation of Chief Nsefu Game Reserve is more complex and well worth telling.

A More Complex Account of Nsefu's Game Reserve

In the late 1920s the British government adopted a new approach to colonial administration which was termed 'indirect rule'. Chief Nsefu's power was derived from this shift in policy. The policy of indirect rule was motivated in part by a desire to help African people to prepare for self-government and independence. It represented also recognition that it was not really feasible for one or two British district officers to conduct the business of government in areas with an average population of 200,000 unless they had some help. Under the system of indirect rule chiefs were expected to act as magistrates, collect taxes and promote economic development. In this they were supported by village headmen and counsellors. The headmen were local people but the counsellors might be educated men who were attracted to the rural areas because decent salaries were paid. So, for example, a man who had worked as a male nurse in the copper mining areas might become a counsellor responsible for health services. Chiefs' salaries varied between six and twenty pounds per year. Chief Nsefu was the paramount chief of the Akunda people and therefore his salary would have been at the higher end of the scale.

Chiefs were not mere automatons, unthinkingly implementing the policy of the Northern Rhodesia government. They tended to behave in accordance with a calculation of what was in their own best interests. Some gave priority to seeking popularity with the people over whom they ruled, e.g. by neglecting to collect the unpopular licence fees on dogs and guns. Others sought to bolster their authority by determinedly co-operating with the district commissioners and provincial commissioner, e.g. in supporting the introduction of cash crops. Many tried to take a middle course. The most effective chiefs built close working relationships with their district commissioners and could rely on them to express local grievances to the authorities in Lusaka.

Chief Nsefu was regarded as a 'progressive' chief by the administrators in Fort Jameson. He had supported the provincial commissioner's scheme to introduce cash crops and had co-operated with the DC, Kenneth Bradley, in encouraging villagers to construct pit latrines. The trouble that Nsefu took to cultivate a good relationship with the British officers may be explained by the vulnerability of his own position. The Akunda were of mixed ethnic origins, the result of inter-marriage between neighbouring peoples. So, it was possible for discontented villagers to say that they regarded themselves as members of another tribe and wanted to divorce themselves from Nsefu. Kenneth Bradley described one such incident in a diary entry for 3 August 1938:

> To-day has been interesting and unusual. It seems that there is a group of villages here whose people have suddenly taken it into their heads to deny allegiance to the Akunda … so I called a camp-fire meeting of all the headmen and Chief Sefu, the leader of the Kunda chiefs, to discuss the affair.
>
> In the course of the argument various old men spoke, and with many digressions and impassioned arguments they led me back through tribal history for a century or more. … [they explained that the name Akunda] … means 'People who have slept with wooden ornaments.' A nasty jibe at their inter-marriage with the Nsenga people. I saw Sefu scowling when I was given this interpretation. The old wound still hurts.
>
> It was obvious from this history and from the discussion that … a change is only desired by a few old men, each of whom thinks he might be given the new chieftainship.
>
> When I told Sefu that they had no case he thanked me prettily by bending on one knee and clapping his hands gently. This is the

> Kunda greeting, and it is curiously dignified. I always have to
> resist an impulse to return the compliment.[34]

By cultivating a good relationship with the British, Nsefu was successful in underpinning his own authority. This was demonstrated when the British cabinet minister for the colonies visited Lusaka in 1949: Nsefu was amongst those introduced to him. A contrasting approach was taken by another chief in the Luangwa Valley, Chief Kakumbi. Kakumbi would appear to have adopted a strategy of dividing the British against one another. According to Major Poles, the game warden based in Mpika, Kakumbi aimed to co-operate with the Provincial Administration whilst doing his utmost to obstruct the Department of Game and Tsetse Control. In July 1947 Poles wrote in his journal an account of a conversation about this with Chief Nsefu:

> We found the paramount chief Ansefu on a visit to the villages.
> He seems a very decent old man with a very intelligent face and
> neat and clean in his person. Had a talk to him. He said that he
> had heard of the trouble that Chief Kakumbi had given me and
> expressed himself as disgusted at his behaviour. Ansefu made
> me a present of a fowl and several eggs and I sent him a puku.[35]

One key factor in Norman Carr's choice of a chief with whom to co-operate in the creation of a game-viewing reserve may well have been his experience in dealing with porters. In 1938, long before Norman was thinking about community-based conservation, he had established a pattern of recruiting his porters from the Akunda tribe. On one occasion he had tried working with a mixed group of Akunda and Awisa porters, but this had culminated in a confrontation that could have resulted in serious trouble. Reflecting on this experience, he wrote

> I usually recruited my carriers from the Akunda people, but on
> this trip I had taken some Wisa from Kambwiri's country and
> these two tribes are traditional enemies. I realised that such a
> situation could become volatile.[36]

The significance of Carr's remarks are underlined by a statement by Zambian historian Samuel Chipungu who says that between 1939 and 1945 several Kambwiri chiefs 'in the neighbourhood of the Luangwa Valley' were deposed by the British authorities for elephant poaching.[37]

By 1945, Nsefu was confirmed in his loyalty to the British and Carr was confirmed in his loyalty to the Akunda. They were natural partners in the project to create a game-viewing reserve. Money provided the final – and conclusive – element in the equation. Visitors to Chief Nsefu's Game Reserve paid an entrance fee of ten shillings. So, if forty visitors came in a single year their entrance fees would be equal to Nsefu's annual salary. In reality, several hundred visitors came each year. Even after allowing for the modest expenses involved in running the rustic camp at Chipera on the bank of the Luangwa, Nsefu's income - and with it his prestige - was massively boosted by the reserve. An additional financial benefit accrued because Nsefu had to enforce the laws on dog and gun licences as part of his commitment to game conservancy. That revenue went into the Native Authority Treasury and was then available to be spent on development projects – new dispensaries, improved roads and bursaries for secondary school pupils. After one year of operation, Nsefu formally applied for his game viewing area to be declared a reserve, so as to protect his new-found interests in conservation.

The success of Chief Nsefu's Game Reserve was noticed by other chiefs. In 1951 Chief Luambe, occupying ground some distance upstream on the same bank of the Luangwa, applied for the creation of Chief Luambe's Game Reserve to be officially sanctioned. This application the authorities were happy to agree. At least two other chiefs took similar initiatives, although it does not appear that they applied for their game reserves to be formally recognised. One of these was on Chisenga Island in Lake Mweru wa Ntipa. It did not prosper. Given that it was not within reasonable driving distance of any major centre of population, this is not surprising. Chief Chinyama, a Barotse [Lozi] chief on the flood plain of the upper Zambezi also created a reserve. The primary problem that he encountered was that his reserve had no effective obstacles to unauthorised entry. White people could and did hunt within the reserve without permission and without making payment and this undermined the financial viability of the scheme. Sir Frank Fraser Darling visited Chief Chinyama in September 1956. The note that he made in his diary is particularly revealing:

> [Chief Chinyama] … told us that Europeans had been over the
> river and had illegally hunted his game in the Reserves, which
> he and his people had set up to conserve the game. … It is really

> very promising that a Chief … should take this step, but …
> Barotseland is not at all like the rest of Northern Rhodesia.[38]

Darling clearly did not know that Chief Chinyama was emulating Chief Nsefu. Nor did Darling have any knowledge of Norman Carr's role in promoting community-based conservation; presumably because his guides, including Eustace Poles, had omitted to give credit where it was due.

The Role of Hunting in Conservation

In 1949 'A scheme for conducting hunting parties, under official auspices, was worked out for the Luangwa Valley, the profits therefrom to be divided equally between government and the native treasury concerned.'[39] This was the second part of Norman Carr's twin-track strategy to protect wildlife on the eastern bank of the Luangwa River. Outside Chief Nsefu's Game Reserve and Chief Luambe's Game Reserve, other chiefs were persuaded to prohibit hunting by local people in a strip of territory extending ten miles from the river bank. In return they were promised half of the licence fees charged to 'big game' hunters.

To promote this scheme, Norman Carr wrote an article 'Elephants in the Eastern Province' for the Northern Rhodesia Journal, a magazine with a large distribution amongst European civil servants, mine workers and other white settlers. He introduced his article with the words 'The following remarks about the distribution and some of the habits of elephant are extracted from notes which I am in the process of compiling … These observations are taken from my field notes written in the course of my duties as a Government Game Ranger.'[40] Unfortunately his field notes no longer exist. In this article Norman argued that the elephant population of the Luangwa Valley was rising and that the average weight of tusks had increased over the previous two decades. By the late 1940s tusks of fifty pounds in weight were regarded as average, seventy to eighty pounds were considered good and anything over one hundred pounds was exceptional.

The Special Game Licences issued under this scheme cost five pounds per person for residents of Northern Rhodesia and twenty pounds for visitors. In addition, payment had to be made for each elephant shot, at the rate of ten pounds for the first and five pounds for each subsequent elephant up to a maximum of four in total. So, each elephant hunter who was resident in Northern Rhodesia would pay a total of thirty pounds in licence fees to shoot four elephants. Given that the prevailing sale price for ivory was fifteen shillings per pound, it is possible to calculate the revenue generated by shooting four elephants with tusks of fifty pounds average weight. This comes to three hundred pounds sterling, an average of seventy-five pounds per elephant. So, a reasonably successful hunter would earn three hundred pounds in a couple of weeks and of this he would pay ten per cent in licence fees. He would be left with two hundred and seventy pounds to defray the cost of travelling to the Luangwa Valley and the cost of hiring and feeding porters, a tracker and a gun bearer. In other words, a proficient hunter could enjoy a fortnight of sport and return home having made money. Norman was careful to emphasise that to achieve this kind of outcome it would be necessary to be patient. The hunter '… will most likely have to turn down many unshootable animals before meeting the heavier tuskers …'.[41] Carr was well placed to offer advice as he supplemented his income each year by taking the necessary licences and patiently hunting for elephants with big tusks. It is reasonable to reckon that by hunting he added more than two hundred pounds to his annual salary of seven hundred and twenty pounds.

In 1950, the first year of the Special Game Licence scheme in the Luangwa Valley '… the two parties which were catered for expressed great satisfaction with the hunting facilities afforded.'[42] If we assume that each party consisted of two hunters and that each of them was licensed to shoot four elephants then the share of revenue due to the chiefs participating in the scheme was sixty pounds – three times the salary payable to a senior chief. In the following year the '…conducted hunting party scheme in the Luangwa Valley was very successful …' and the number of hunting parties increased.[43] Norman Carr argued that the scheme was successful in achieving its aims.

> It was obligatory that all meat from these safaris except that consumed in camp should go to the local people. The take-off of animals from safari hunting was … infinitesimal compared with the natural increase and the scheme did protect the vital river area. Any hardship that might have resulted from the loss of hunting privileges was negligible because the people received their meat anyway …[44]

Chapter 6

Legislation and Suppression of Poaching

Leave in 1950

In 1950, the Carr family went to South Africa on leave. Norman was reluctant to go because his work with Chief Nsefu was important to him. However, Barbara insisted that the poor state of her children's health made it essential. Their son Adrian was a small baby, so they went to the coast near Durban rather than undertake the much longer journey to the UK. Norman's younger sister, Cecily, joined the family in South Africa and so did his mother-in-law. The family stayed for a prolonged period. Adrian learned to walk there, and Judy went to school. Barbara recruited a nanny called Dorothy who came with them to Chilanga when the leave was over. Norman reported for duty at the Game Department's HQ in Chilanga in mid-October.

Legislation

New legislation was being prepared in the Game Department. Three separate ordinances had to be drafted along with explanatory memoranda. These dealt with the game laws, national parks, and fisheries. The first two were of special interest to Norman. It is possible that a high degree of premeditation and planning had gone into Norman's appointment as Acting Assistant Director of the Game Department. Ordinarily, the work of drafting new legislation would have been led or, at least, overseen by the director of the department most directly concerned with the subject matter. Work on the Fauna Conservation Ordinance, in stark contrast, commenced soon after the Director, Vaughan-Jones, had left for eight months leave. It is plausible to argue that the Governor Sir Gilbert Rennie and his Chief Secretary R C S Stanley had waited until Vaughan-Jones was due to depart and then sent in Norman Carr as a carefully selected alternative leader for the drafting process. Stanley would have read Carr's file and knew that he had previously worked for the Attorney General in Nyasaland. This departure from established custom and practice was explained blandly with the words '... posted to Headquarters at the end of his leave to assist in the absence of the Director ...'[45]

There was a wide range of parties interested in the Fauna Conservation Ordinance. In drafting both legislation and explanatory memoranda, Norman had to keep their varying priorities and concerns in mind. He also had to make astute judgements on matters of substance, presentation, and tactics. It is worth making an effort to identify some of the main interested parties and to consider their concerns.

The first interested party was the government of Northern Rhodesia: the governor, chief secretary and Executive Council. Their task was not an easy one: they were simultaneously accountable to the British government and Parliament in London and to the Legislative Assembly in Lusaka which, for much of the 1950s, was dominated by white settler politicians. In 1950 Sir Gilbert Rennie was governor and Mr (later Sir) Robert Stanley was chief secretary. Both men were in their 50s and had devoted their adult lives to the colonial service. A primary concern for them was the maintenance of public order and the avoidance of politically motivated disturbances. Rennie had been awarded the Military Cross whilst serving in an infantry regiment during the First World War. After studying at Glasgow University, he had joined the colonial service in 1920 and been posted to Ceylon (Sri Lanka). Immediately before his appointment as governor of Northern Rhodesia in December 1947, Rennie had been chief secretary in Kenya. One of the principal duties of all chief secretaries was to act as head of the civil service. Chief secretaries were responsible for promotions, transfers and discipline and usually took a close interest in individual officers. As chief secretary of Northern Rhodesia in the early 1950s, Robert Stanley was Governor Rennie's right-hand man. He had served in Africa for about 30 years and was later rewarded for his work with Rennie by being appointed as high commissioner for Britain's colonial territories in the Western Pacific. More will be said below about the role of Rennie and Stanley in shaping legislation on game conservation.

The level of nationalist activity was low in 1950/51. However, as the ordinance passed through the legislative process and the challenges of implementation had to be dealt with in detail, the political background changed. In the run-up to the creation of the Federation of Rhodesia and Nyasaland in 1953 there was a rising tide of African nationalism and a clear danger that local grievances might be used for political purposes. By the mid-1950s the governor and his senior colleagues knew they must face the need to clear the human population out of part of the Zambezi Valley as the flood waters of the Kariba Dam rose. The dam was one of the Federation's most prestigious projects and would supply power to industry and urban settlements, but at a high price to some rural Africans. Sir Arthur Benson who took over as governor in May 1954 anticipated disturbances in the Gwembe Valley and was anxious to avoid similar problems elsewhere. Norman Carr was on good terms with Benson who had provided much needed hospitality whilst Norman was on safari in the wet season in the late 1930s when Benson had been an assistant DC in the Northern Province.

The provincial administration is worth considering separately from the government. This group consisted of the provincial commissioners and district commissioners and they constituted the first point of contact between the government and the population. A primary concern for them was the prospect that in many areas shooting of game had become unsustainable. They saw themselves as protectors of indigenous people. Many DCs feared that in future people would no longer have game meat as a source of protein because antelopes etc would be exterminated. So, they tended to favour game laws that would restrain but not outlaw hunting by Africans. They were not usually keen on national parks from which local people would be totally excluded.

The chiefs were traditional rulers who held power outside the urban areas. They had widely varying agendas in which their own interests and the interests of their peoples (as articulated by village headmen and tribal councillors) were key factors. Some had used game reserves to generate substantial income – including Chief Nsefu whose experience has been referred to above. Some were reluctant to enforce the existing licensing laws in relation to dogs and guns as enforcement made them unpopular. Others saw revenue from enforcing the licensing laws as a valuable source of funding for development purposes. Some changed their position over time. Whilst chiefs were emphatically not mere puppets of the colonial government, nor yet were they entirely at liberty to do as they pleased. For example, in the 1940s Chief Chipepo of Broken Hill rural district was deposed for illegal elephant hunting and embezzlement. Similar episodes occurred elsewhere including the Luangwa Valley.

Settlers had a special role in influencing legislation, both through the Game Preservation and Hunting Association of Northern Rhodesia and by virtue of their representation on the Legislative Council. Some of the settlers tended to articulate notions of sportsmanship that had echoes of hunting with hounds in Britain. Many were particularly anxious about the large number of firearms held by Africans. This reflected concerns created by Mau Mau in Kenya as well as ideas about game conservation. They tended to advocate strong command and control measures including the creation of national parks as total exclusion zones and the disarmament of the local people. Like the chiefs, settlers were a varied group. The farmers amongst them were particularly concerned with tsetse control and supported the eradication of wildlife in control zones to prevent the spread of sleeping sickness in domestic livestock which is transmitted by tsetse flies. Prominent amongst the settlers was Mrs Erica Lafone, a member of the Legislative Council. She was unusual as an opponent of hunting in all its forms, including licensed big game hunting. With her second husband, Lt-Col Critchley, she ran the Blue Lagoon Ranch on the Kafue Flats as a game sanctuary, particularly to protect the red lechwe, a species of water antelope.

The Fauna Society in London was able to exert influence in subtle ways, not least by lobbying the Colonial Office where senior officials and ministers were on first-name terms with the Society's figures. The role of metropolitan conservation groups in shaping policy in the colonial setting is reflected quite accurately in one of the adventures of the fictional James Bond – 007. In Ian Fleming's novel *Dr No* the Audubon Society in the USA seeks to protect a population of roseate spoonbills both by direct intervention and by pressuring the colonial government of Jamaica. When the Society's wardens are murdered, Bond is dispatched to investigate. In Northern Rhodesia the situation was less dramatic, but the Game Preservation and Hunting Association was able to influence policy by getting influential figures in the Fauna Society in Britain to lobby on their behalf. A similar situation prevailed in relation to Kenya. It seems likely that some senior people in the colonial service shared the outlook of the fictional head of the Secret Service, M:

> The trouble is these sort of people get really worked up about
> their damned birds or whatever it is. They get the politicians
> involved. And somehow they all seem to have stacks of money.
> God knows where it comes from. Other old women, I suppose.[46]

The Game and Tsetse Control Department in which Norman worked occupied a pivotal position. The prevailing ethos of the department was one of command and control. Sir Frank Fraser Darling noticed this when he visited as an ecological consultant in 1956. He spent time with Major Eustace Poles, an exceptionally brave man who had led guerrilla activities in Eastern Burma in wartime. Poles insisted on game guards saluting, marching on parade, and maintaining their kit in a military manner. Darling noted in his diary that Poles called Africans 'munts', a term that had once been used simply to mean 'people' but which had acquired overtones of racial prejudice. Most members of the Game Department's staff were supporters both of national parks from which local people would be totally excluded and of complete bans on hunting by Africans using guns and dogs.

Norman Carr's position was a subtle and sophisticated one. He was eager to secure the legal position of community-based conservation initiatives run by Nsefu, Luambe and others and the Special Game Licence scheme. At the same time, he was concerned also to secure active engagement with the Game Preservation and Hunting Association. He recognised that the presence of licensed white hunters in the bush had a significant deterrent impact on poaching and he was a supporter of enlisting members of the GPHA as honorary game wardens. Overall, he was seeking a legal regime that would eschew strong command and control measures in favour of building the active cooperation of indigenous peoples. In this he was aligning himself with the governor, chief secretary, and other top brass. He seems to have believed that he (and they) had been largely successful. In his book *The White Impala'* he wrote:

> When I look back on a lifetime spent mostly in or on the fringes
> of wildlife sanctuaries in Africa, I feel I must try and draw up
> a mental balance sheet. In one column I must put the loss of
> human companionship ... [and] those phases early in my career
> when hunting became an obsession and I killed more elephants

> and buffalo than was absolutely necessary ... On the other hand,
> I think I should give myself credit for my part in the formation of
> several sanctuaries ... [and] *I have helped to draft legislation and*
> *influence new policies ...*[47]

Norman had support from above in his work on legislation. After the Game Department's Director, Vaughan-Jones, had returned from leave he was made aware that the Governor and Chief Secretary approved of Norman's drafts and expected Vaughan-Jones to do the same. The Minister of Agriculture, Beckett, had responsibility for the Game Department and he made a speech publicly endorsing the draft ordinances. Major Poles observed 'V-J finding a powerful wind on his beam is scudding gracefully before it – Beckett's pennant indicating its direction.'[48] In due course, Vaughan-Jones was rewarded with promotion to the post of Commissioner for Rural Development. Norman, with Vaughan-Jones's support, prepared the agenda for a crucial conference on the draft new ordinances held in Chilanga between 5 and 8 February 1952. This was attended by most of the department's senior staff. Norman ensured that the agenda was long and that there was plenty to talk about in the plenary sessions. In addition, two committees were set up: one on elephant control; and the other on standardisation of equipment and centralisation of stores. There was a raft of lively social activities too which often went on late into the night. As a result, the attendees dispersed having talked a great deal, expressed their views at length and having had a thoroughly good time but without reaching any firm conclusions that might have impeded Norman in achieving his objectives.

The Fauna Conservation Ordinance was brought into force in 1954. Fifty years later, in a retrospective assessment, Bill Astles – who had served in the Game Department and went on to work for the Food and Agriculture Organisation of the UN - judged that the ordinance had been a success. In his judgement, following the implementation of indirect rule in the inter-war years, there was a binary divide between game reserves and other areas. In game reserves hunting was prohibited. Villagers living inside game reserves could choose to remain, but no crop protection was provided. Outside game reserves local people could hunt. Chiefs were supposed to issue licences and enforce limitations on the number of animals killed. Astles argues that whilst some did issue licences (as a source of revenue) enforcement was minimal. In essence, most villagers simply wanted all wild animals killed because they raided crops or competed for grazing. He goes on to argue that the Game Ordinance of 1941 reflected the hope that chiefs would recognise meat from hunting as a valuable source of protein and manage wildlife in a sustainable way. By the late 1940s it had become apparent that, overall, this was not working. The Fauna Conservation Ordinance of 1954 replaced the controlled areas with 16 First Class Controlled Hunting Areas where the rules would be enforced by the Game Department. The rules provided for a closed season and included a prohibition on the hunting of nursing females. The First Class Controlled Hunting Areas extended to 421,025 sq. km. In them, the Game Department determined quotas: the portion allocated to indigenous residents was allocated by the chiefs through licences and enforcement was by the Game Department. The remaining licences were controlled by the Game Department and included professional hunters' permits.

The Fauna Conservation Ordinance of 1954 was a necessarily complex piece of legislation. Key features, beyond the provisions relating to First Class Controlled Hunting Areas, may be summarised as follows. Hunting in Game Reserves was prohibited, except for culling. Private Game Areas could be created on privately owned land. This was to prove important in the conservation of lechwe on the Kafue Flats. Honorary game rangers could be appointed with the powers of game officers. Some animals were protected and could not be hunted. These included cheetahs, eland, giraffe, hippos, females of several smaller antelopes, rhinos and a range of birds including those that eat locusts. A range of hunting methods were declared unlawful. These prohibitions do not explicitly distinguish between Africans and Europeans. However, the following bans appear to be aimed at Africans primarily – gin traps, game pits, stakes, poison and driving animals into water. Those aimed at Europeans primarily, included the prohibition of the use of automatic weapons, bulala lamps and hunting from vehicles. There was a prohibition on night hunting too which appears to be colour-blind. Exemptions could be granted 'to accord with native customs', so a *chila* could be permitted.

Whilst they were living in Chilanga, Norman happily extended hospitality to colleagues in the game department. It is likely that he would have done this in any circumstances but it was particularly important, during the period that the draft legislation was under discussion, that he should cultivate good personal relationships with colleagues who might not be wholly supportive of his efforts to shape the ordinance. Whilst Vaughan-Jones was on leave the Carrs lived in his house. This provided an ideal location for parties and impromptu social gatherings. This pattern of open-handed entertainment infuriated Barbara. She knew that, although Norman temporarily held the title of Acting Assistant Director, he received neither additional salary nor any entertainment allowance. In fact, Norman's salary of £865 was not really adequate to keep a family with three children, even though Norman paid no income tax. Barbara had had to take what she considered a dreary and disagreeable job in the Public Works Department in Lusaka to enable the family to pay its bills. To make matters worse, Mrs Vaughan-Jones had locked away some of the better furniture in rooms that Barbara was not permitted to enter: nonetheless, Norman was paying the rent for the house in full. Matters came to a head when Barbara's car broke down one evening on the journey home from Lusaka. After hours of waiting, a passing mechanic helped her. Norman failed to come and look for her because he was busy entertaining game rangers whom she described caustically as: 'a pert little man in a ridiculous cowboy outfit, crawling on all fours… [and] … a brawny giant with a cauliflower ear and an aboriginal brow …'[49]

Ndola and Luapula

In 1952, a few months after the Chilanga conference on game legislation, Norman and Barbara Carr moved to Ndola, a large city on the rapidly developing Copperbelt. He was promoted to rank of assistant game warden and his salary increased to £900 per annum. The following year he was promoted again to chief ranger. Barbara too received a pay rise when she moved to the Public Works Department office in Ndola, from £370 to £415. Norman and Barbara were allocated a brand-new bungalow with electricity, running water, a flush toilet, and a telephone. There were schools in Ndola for their children, a government hospital and shops selling an abundance of imported goods – even books. This should have been a change for the better. The reality was not so rosy.

In order to understand why Norman's position in Ndola was challenging, it is necessary to provide some context, starting with changes in the mining industry during the Second World War. The war had increased demand for copper substantially. Copper was a strategic material. It was essential for electrical wiring, not least in engines of all kinds and sizes. It was used also in munitions: the brass shell casings used by the artillery on land and the Royal Navy at sea contained copper. The copper companies responded to this by increasing output, both to support the war effort and to make money. However, they encountered serious difficulties in terms of industrial relations.

At the outbreak of war, many men of British origin had left the copper mining industry to join the armed forces. Among them were electricians, plumbers, ventilation engineers, crane drivers, locomotive engineers, and other skilled artisans. The companies had to replace them and recruited heavily amongst Afrikaners from South Africa. Consequently, the Europeans-only Northern Rhodesia Mine Workers Union [NRMWU] came under the control of people who were actively hostile to the British Empire and to the British war effort. Strike action became commonplace, and no sooner were pay rises conceded than fresh demands were made. African mine workers, who had no properly organised trade union, observed what was happening and made demands of their own. These culminated in violence against non-striking mine workers and rioting. On one occasion the rioting threatened key installations including shaft winding engines and troops opened fire. Meanwhile, leaflets were circulating amongst white mine workers advocating an armed insurrection. There was a clear danger that the production of copper might be disrupted.

The government's response to the tense situation on the Copperbelt in the early 1940s depended on two men, neither of whom were colonial civil servants. One was Sir Stewart Gore-Browne, a planter with a large estate at Shiwa Ngandu in the Bemba country. Sir Stewart bravely went into the main African township at Nkana and persuaded the strikers to return to work on the basis that their grievances would be investigated and rectified. The other key figure was Roy Welensky, leader of the Europeans-only railwaymen's union. Welensky described himself as fifty per cent Lithuanian, fifty per cent Jewish and one hundred per cent British. He had been a locomotive engineer and a boxing champion. Welensky accepted office as wartime director of manpower and arranged for the most anti-British leaders of the NRMWU to be arrested in dawn raids on 6 October 1942 and interned without trial. This drastic action stabilised the situation. With everybody back at work, the mining companies' revenues soared.

Their workforce – black and white - became by far the best paid in Northern Rhodesia. As mentioned above, government revenues rocketed and this made possible the creation of the Game Department.

When the war ended, prosperity continued. Copper prices remained high well into the 1960s, although with occasional set-backs. Mine workers of all races continued to earn extraordinarily large sums of money. Government revenues continued to benefit. Nonetheless, both industrial relations and race relations on the Copperbelt were tense and sometimes confrontational. The NRMWU imposed a colour-bar in the copper mines. They did this in a sophisticated way, by insisting that an African worker who undertook any part of an artisan's work must receive the full payment due to the artisan. So, any African worker who did the simplest form of electrical work - wiring a plug or replacing a damaged cable, must be paid the same rate of pay as a European electrician. This was presented as an equal pay policy. Really the policy served to exclude Africans from skilled work. Meanwhile, with the Labour Party in office in Britain, the African mine workers were sent a British trade unionist to help them set up their own union – the Northern Rhodesia African Mine Workers Union [NRAMWU]. This rapidly became a formidable force, well able to function without external support.

Ndola was on the Eastern end of the Copperbelt. The main mining operations took place further west in Chingola, Kitwe, Luanshya, and Mufulira. In Ndola there were some mining company surface activities, such as refining. In addition, there were many companies that provided services to the mining industry and its workforce. These included civil engineering, construction, motor maintenance, food wholesale and even agricultural support firms. The railways had a big presence also. In terms of the salaries and wages paid, there was a hierarchy with the mining companies at the top, service companies in the middle and the public sector at the bottom. Norman and Barbara had a joint income of £1,315 a year. By comparison, at this time white men in their early 20s who had recently completed apprenticeships and started work as craftsmen in the mining industry were being paid £2,000. The wives of mine workers and other private sector employees had lots of money to spend. Many of them even had ostentatiously expensive cars. The wives of civil servants had to be careful with money. Barbara commented, with characteristic bitterness, 'We of the government huddled in our derelict houses … and tried to pretend that we were … very much more important … than our flashy, rich neighbours in the nearby mining towns …'[50]

Norman faced two complex challenges in his working life. Firstly, the relatively high disposable incomes available to African mine workers generated a high level of demand for bush meat provided by poachers. Secondly, some European mine workers delighted in poaching as a means of defying authority. No European mine worker went poaching out of necessity. They could well afford to pay for game licences. Indeed, many of the clients travelling to the Luangwa Valley under the Special Game Licence scheme came from the Copperbelt: by doing so they generated income for African chiefs and their people.

The challenge from European poachers came primarily from anti-British Afrikaners who possessed reliable, accurate rifles. One significant barrier to their activities was self-inflicted. It was their choice of cars. Expensive gas-guzzler cars imported from the United States were a status symbol amongst white artisans working in and around the mines. Characteristically these cars were long, gaudily decorated with dazzling arrays of chrome and had a low clearance. It was the low clearance that made them ill-suited to travel on dirt roads in the bush, even in dry weather. Once the remaining animals within reach of the tarred road network on the Copperbelt had been hunted almost to extinction, the white poachers turned to a new technique. This was to hunt by night and to lure animals towards them by using lamps. In October 1953 three Europeans – all Afrikaners - were convicted of breaking the game laws by shooting large numbers of buck at night using Bulala lamps which they wore fitted to their heads like the lamps used by miners underground. The powerful light from the lamp was described as causing antelopes to stand still, making them easy targets. Each of the men was fined £100.

Norman had one great source of support in his work in and around the Copperbelt, in the form of honorary game rangers. These were senior men, mostly from the mines, who spent a good deal of time in the bush. They included graduate engineers, geologists, industrial chemists, metallurgists, surveyors and (from the Roan Antelope Company in Luanshya) its most senior personnel (human resources) manager and its director of Medical Services. Few poachers – black or white – would dare disobey orders given by these men.

Whilst based in Ndola, Norman was responsible for the Luapula Province as well as the Copperbelt. The Luapula Province was quite different from the Copperbelt in that it was quintessential bush country, accessed by driving across what was then Belgian territory in the Congo's 'Pedicle'. It included Lake Mweru Wantipa (sometimes called Mweru Marsh), close to the Congo border, and Lake Mweru itself which was officially cut in half by the border. The western fringes of Lake Bangweulu were also within Norman's area, although the main responsibility for that lake lay with a colleague based in Mpika. There was just one small town in Luapula Province, at Fort Rosebery (now Mansa), where the provincial commissioner had his office. Norman had previously spent several months in this area whilst working as a crop protection officer in 1938/39. In the interim, things had changed. Now his main task was to detect and deter the trade in illicit bush meat, much of which went to the mines in Belgian territory.

Barbara joined Norman on just one tour of duty in the Luapula Province and her account of this is worth quoting at length:

> From Ndola I did one tour with Norman to Mweru Marsh on the … border. One of the purposes was to work out a compromise between the needs of the natives … whose livelihood depended on the fishing and saltmaking, and the game in the reserve surrounding it … Our route followed the shores of the Marsh for the next week. The belt of vegetation consisted almost entirely of 'Mateshi' thicket … there were game tracks formed by generations of elephant and buffalo … [a] … labyrinth of passages and tunnels winding through the dense thicket … We saw a few timid klipspringers which bounced away as soon as they caught sight of us … Norman brought them to a standstill by giving a shrill whistle which made them halt in full flight and turn round curiously. This weakness makes them an easy target[51]

Uncharacteristically, Norman made a mistake in siting their tent and campfire one night during this foot safari. As a result, the smoke from the fire blew into their tent. Barbara added 'I had a temperature of 104 degrees and the experience was particularly unpleasant'[52]

Leave in 1953

In 1953, the Carr family went to Britain on leave. This should have been a chance to repair a marriage that was fraying around the edges, but the overall result was to make matters worse. Norman was reluctant to go because his work was the source of deep satisfaction to him. However, the poor condition of his two daughters, Pam and Judy, and his infant son, Adrian, made it necessary. They all had an unhealthy yellow skin tone as the result of taking anti-malarial drugs and they were underweight. Eight months leave was granted because the journey by rail and sea to Britain via Cape Town was a long and arduous one. In Bulawayo, a major rail hub, they were met by Norman's sister Eve who provided some welcome hospitality. They arrived in England in the Spring. They leased accommodation from a Mr & Mrs Dawkins in Essex who specialised in renting to colonial officers on leave. As mentioned in the previous chapter, Norman devoted one month to a course in Zoology at the University of London. Subsequently he returned to London for three weeks to join a team at the Zoological Society's Regents Park Zoo undertaking scientific research on animals. The family took a holiday in the Fort William area in North-Western Scotland which did little to promote marital harmony. Whilst Norman enthused over the mountain air and wild scenery, Barbara complained about the damp weather and remoteness from urban delights. Eventually she had four weeks in which to dash around art galleries, department stores and book shops whilst Norman entertained the children in parks. Barbara was looking forward to another six weeks of metropolitan culture when Norman insisted on returning to Northern Rhodesia early.

The reason Norman was keen to return was that he had planned to do some work with Chief Nsefu in the Luangwa Valley. This was un-official and unpaid and had to be completed before he reported back for duty in Ndola.

Ill-health and Early Retirement

Barbara's health problems came to a head during 1953. She became seriously ill, but the government doctors offered neither diagnosis nor sick leave from her duties in the Public Works Department. Barbara contacted her mother by telegram and her mother drove 1,000 miles from Zomba to provide support, not least with child-care. When Norman returned from the bush, he took Barbara to a private clinic. Here they were advised to go to a clinic in Johannesburg without delay for further examination and testing. Norman asked the provincial medical officer to sanction this. After three weeks of waiting, and in the absence of any response from the provincial medical officer, Norman decided to take Barbara regardless. 'To fly in the face of government orders was asking a great deal of a man steeped in government procedure but … he bravely took me off.'[53] She was diagnosed as having thyrotoxicosis due to an overactive thyroid gland. This required treatment with radio-active iodine which was available in Johannesburg and London but not in Northern Rhodesia. Norman and Barbara agreed that she and their children should re-locate to Johannesburg where treatment for her and good schooling for the children was available. This would keep them within travelling distance of Norman.

The apparent incompetence of the government's medical service calls for a brief explanation. The Colonial Medical Service was focussed on public health services for the benefit of the African population and regarded providing curative services for European civil servants and their families as a distraction from this primary purpose. Doctors recruited to the Colonial Medical Service were required to spend the whole of their first home leave in studying for the Diploma in Public Health. Thereafter, promotion depended on achievements in vaccination and inoculation campaigns, hygiene improvements and infant health education programmes. This was in sharp contrast to the mining companies on the Copperbelt which employed first class surgeons and experienced family practitioners. In some colonial territories, including Aden and Tanganyika, good surgeons from India were employed to work alongside the Colonial Medical Service. That Northern Rhodesia did not adopt that practice was to have serious consequences for Norman.

Norman continued with his routine of prolonged tours around the Copperbelt and Luapula provinces, trying to persuade chiefs and tribal elders of the harm that poaching caused and simultaneously to deter poaching. Then, in August 1955 he was gored by a buffalo. The buffalo had no interest in eating him – they are not carnivores. It succeeded in penetrating Norman's lower back and pushed a horn inside his rib cage from behind. Then he threw Norman into the air. Norman was taken to the Government Hospital in Ndola and operated on. The operation was botched, he was left in considerable pain and with limited mobility. After a lengthy recuperation period, it was decided that Norman could no longer carry out his duties as a game warden and he was retired on half pay. The Game and Tsetse Control Department's annual report for 1955 opened with a tribute to him which stated

> A severe loss was sustained during the year through the retirement on grounds of ill-health of Mr N. J. Carr, Chief Ranger. Mr Carr joined the Department ... in 1939 ,.. so was virtually a 'foundation member'. In the period of rapid post-war expansion his experience and ability proved invaluable, and his loss will be keenly felt. He was awarded the M.B.E. in the 1956 New Year's Honours'[54]

Norman joined Barbara in their flat at 15 Rosebank Mansions, Oxford Road, Johannesburg. He maintained a vestigial attachment to the Game Department by enlisting as an honorary game ranger. In Johannesburg Norman underwent a second operation on his back. This was more successful than the previous one and gradually he regained his mobility. Finding it difficult to spend time indoors in a flat, he developed the habit of passing much of the day in public parks. To help occupy his time, he started writing about his experiences in animal conservation, although he did not publish his writings at this time. Barbara had to earn more money, to keep their finances balanced, so she qualified as a secretary before eventually becoming an estate agents' saleswoman.

Norman does not appear to have looked back on his time in Ndola with any great fondness. Although he published several books, the only occasion that he mentioned Ndola in any of them was to refer in passing to the shade trees planted at the side of the road by the City Council.

Chapter 7

Kafue National Park

Introduction

Norman Carr returned from Johannesburg in August 1957 to become the warden of the Kafue National Park. Although less eye-catching than the Luangwa Valley, the Park had much to recommend it. Ian Manning enthused over it, writing, 'The Kafue is a paradise of floodplain, forest, thicket, dambo and marsh with a greater variety of game than the Luangwa'.[55] Norman had been asked to come back because the National Park had not been developed as originally intended and its management was a mess. Norman was appointed as a temporary local recruit with no overseas leave entitlements and an annual salary of £1,710. He continued to draw a pension of about £500, so overall he was better off than ever before. His boss was F. I. Parnell, a Cambridge graduate who had previously worked in Bechuanaland (Botswana) and had held the position of deputy director before taking over as director of the Game Department in December 1955.

Problems

The Kafue National Park was large. At 8,650 square miles it was two and a half times bigger than the South Luangwa Game Reserve (now National Park). It was a curiously shaped park, 180 miles from the southern boundary to the Busanga Plain and swamps in the north but nowhere more than 100 miles from east to west. However, it did not include the Kafue Flats on which a substantial population of red lechwe lived. The Park was declared in April 1950, and it was announced that during a five-year development period the public would not be able to visit. Unfortunately, the Park was not put on a sound legal footing at the outset. Instead of passing an ordinance to transfer the land to the Crown, it was assumed that the whole area was virtually uninhabited and that the few existing African residents could readily be relocated, or alternatively, that they would coexist harmoniously with the Park.

Vaughan-Jones, Director of the Game Department, compounded the problems inherent in failing to sort out the Park's legal status by appointing L.E. Vaughan to be in charge. Len Vaughan was an amiable person but neither a strong character nor adept at putting the resident African population at their ease in conversation. To compound the position, he had inadequate project management skills.

Vaughan tried to adopt a confrontational and authoritarian approach with the Ila and other African people who were scattered in small numbers across and around the Park. This was ill-advised because he did not possess a sufficiently large staff of game guards to enforce his commands. To make matters worse, when he asked the police and district commissioners to send in policemen and district messengers to help establish his authority, they were reluctant to help. As the Park did not stand on Crown land, the police were not confident that there was any basis on which they might arrest the villagers. By exposing an insufficient force of game guards to the defiance of local people, Vaughan undermined both the game guards' authority and his own.

The ritual buffalo hunt, *chila*, held by Ila men on the fringes of the Busanga Plain towards the end of each dry season was a major source of friction. When Norman served as the game ranger based in Kasempa in 1943/44 he had witnessed the hunt. However, he did not participate. He viewed it as an established African custom that helped to keep ancient traditional values alive. He had reckoned that fifty buffalo had been killed out of approximately 2,000 on the plains. Barbara accompanied him and her response was quite different. It is worth quoting at length:

> The previous night the tribesmen had taken part in what was called a 'dance of courage'.... As we stood on our high anthill I watched the plain rustle .... I could see the black backs of the buffalo moving slowly .... All around the plain ... drums began to beat out .... In the far distance a column of smoke rose.The senior man has just fired the grass after their prayer to the spirits for the hunters to have 'straight spears and stout hearts' said the

game guard with us. The drums are silent while the elders call on the spirits of those who have died bravely on previous hunts to enter the bodies of those about to challenge the buffalo.

The spears were hurled haphazardly and no buffalo died swiftly .... The bellows of the crazed beasts and the thudding of their hoofs as they stampeded ... and the blood curdling yells of the natives made me block my ears.... The ghastly hunt went on all day and by late afternoon the scene was one of tragedy and desolation .... I returned home ... disillusioned, nauseated and revolted.[56]

By October 1951 the situation regarding the Ila buffalo hunt had developed. Not only did the provincial commissioner and several of his staff attend, as Norman had done, they actively participated, using rifles. Given that this was the case, and that hunters gored during the hunt were treated in the Government Hospital, it is understandable that the Ila tribal leaders believed they had the government's endorsement. So, when Vaughan tried to ban the hunt, he encountered both bafflement and resistance.

Construction works – road making, bridge building, the establishment of camps from which game guards could patrol, and of camps intended for tourists - was desperately slow in the years between 1950 and 1952. In fairness to Vaughan, it should be acknowledged that there were two factors which made his work challenging: the geographical distribution of his colleagues; and communications. Vaughan's base (when not in the bush) was the boma at Namwala. The designated Park HQ was at Ngoma, where the road from Namwala crossed the Park's eastern boundary. Vaughan was supposed to be coordinating his activities with game rangers based in Mumbwa and Kasempa. As late as 1956, a routine method of communicating from Ngoma Camp was for written messages to be carried by a runner on foot to Namwala, then taken by van to the Game Department's HQ in Chilanga, then by van to Mumbwa or Kasempa. If the game warden from Mumbwa or Kasempa was out in the bush, then a runner would carry the message to him. This process could take a week – as could any reply. As a result, coordination was poor.

Vaughan should have started his work by making a road from north to south that would have enabled internal communications inside the Park. Had he done this then messages could have been sent in a Land Rover to his colleagues by the shortest possible route. In addition, he could have concentrated the game guards when he needed a show of force, and dispersed them in the bush when that was called for. In practice, Vaughan concentrated on the area around Ngoma. He relied on his colleague in Kasempa to create roads and camps for visitors in the north, whilst his colleague in Mumbwa was expected to mount anti-poaching patrols along part of the eastern boundary. Much of the work done was of a temporary seasonal nature. Although the clearance of trees to make way for roads represented a long-term achievement, many of the dirt roads created in 1950 had to be remade in 1951 and again in 1952 following the rains.

During 1953, Rhodes centenary celebrations had the effect of diverting Vaughan away from all other duties. The Northern Rhodesia government decided that, as they had received reports from Vaughan which painted a picture of good steady progress, they would invite VIP guests to visit Kafue National Park in August and September as part of the celebrations. However, Vaughan's reports on objectives achieved in 1950-2 had been misleading and exaggerated. Faced with the possibility that he might be detected in making false reports, he diverted all available resources into preparations for the VIPs. To minimise the risk of being caught out, he declared the game viewing areas in the north of the Park to be 'out of bounds' and then concentrated on Ngoma camp and the area to the south of it.

In 1952 Vaughan had reported that slow progress in developing the road network was due to damage by elephant herds. This was an odd claim and might have prompted the director, to wonder whether Vaughan's choice of routes was at fault. [It should be added for the sake of clarity that Vaughan, the warden, and Vaughan-Jones, the director, were not blood relatives.] Equally oddly, Vaughan had reported in 1951 that there was virtually no poaching in the Park, and yet in the following year he claimed that poaching was decreasing. These were obviously inconsistent statements. The veracity of Vaughan's reports was further called into question in a radio broadcast on 23 November 1952. In her broadcast on game preservation, Mrs Erica Lafone, a member of the Legislative Assembly, asserted that there were 1,000 African residents in the southern parts of the Park. She added that they had so many guns that there was a gunsmith living in the park to keep them in working order. Nevertheless, the director accepted Vaughan's 'Rome was not built in a day' explanations and provided him with an assistant game ranger: E. O. Charlton, who had served in the Royal Air Force, was appointed.

By 1953, the director was in a tricky position. He had incorporated misleading reports of progress into his department's annual reports. The government in Lusaka had summarised these in their reports to the Colonial Office in London. And the Colonial Office had put them into their publications. To admit that all was not well would have caused embarrassment and that might have jeopardised his promotion prospects.

Between 1954 and 1956 substantial buildings were constructed at Ngoma, the Park's HQ. These were built by the Public Works Department and took the form of rectangular concrete and glass structures with metal window frames. They cost £48,000 – a large chunk of the total budget – and were not at all the kind of accommodation that most tourists liked. The main 'rest house' was brutally ugly; it was also poorly ventilated, suffocating in hot weather, and ill-designed to exclude mosquitoes and other insects. It was jokingly christened the 'Gin palace' – a reference to the Djinn Palace in Kenya which was a haunt of the louche 'Happy Valley' set. The two-roomed and four-roomed chalets for family groups were not much better than the main building. When Sir Frank Fraser Darling visited the Park in 1956, he insisted that a temporary tented camp should be set up for his use because he would not use the 'rest house'.

For three years, from 1954 Ngoma Camp and the area to the south of it were closed, whilst the Public Works Department undertook construction at Ngoma. Visitors were permitted to visit the northern part of the Park via Kasempa and, by 1955 a chain of small camps had been constructed to accommodate them. In 1956 heavy rains made access via Kasempa difficult and only three camps could be made fit for use and re-opened. Parties of school children – mostly European and African pupils from the Copperbelt – visited.

In 1955 an Advisory Board for Kafue National Park was set up. The members included men who held responsible senior positions in major business companies. They were instrumental in having the Park reorganised. A post of game warden was created, and it was agreed that the person appointed to that position would have three European subordinates and some senior, experienced game guards. All of them were to work out of the HQ at Ngoma. Vaughan was not offered the warden's job. Instead he was quietly moved to other duties. In fact, the position of warden remained vacant for over a year. Apparently, most staff of the Game Department regarded it as a poisoned chalice – a posting that could destroy the appointee's career.

The Advisory Board also tackled the question of the Park's legal standing. On 26 April 1956, Harry Grenfell, local secretary of the British South Africa Company wrote from his office in Lusaka to the secretary of state for the colonies. The secretary of state was Alan Lennox Boyd: he and Grenfell were on first name terms. Grenfell argued, on behalf of the Advisory Board, that the current status of the Park did not meet the requirements of the 1933 International Fauna Convention. He urged that the land should be conveyed in perpetuity to a Board of Trustees. This issue would remain unresolved until 1961.[57]

Solutions

Norman Carr was an ideal person to fill the job of warden of Kafue National Park. At school in Britain he had learnt accountancy, formal communication techniques, and good record keeping. These provided the foundations for good project management and budget control. As head of the Confidential Registry in the Secretariat of the Government of Nyasaland he had gained valuable insights into how colonial government worked in practice. Since joining the Game Department in 1943, he had demonstrated a capacity for innovation and had shown tact and empathy in establishing relationships with African people and their leaders.

Carr's position in relation to budget and staffing was a privileged one. In 1957-8 copper prices had fallen by a third and government revenues had fallen with them. Major economies were imposed on the Game Department. In 1958, the number of game rangers was reduced from nineteen to nine and the number of game guards from 348 to 237. Of the total of nine game rangers in the whole country, three were employed in the Park and a fourth was stationed in Kasempa and played a critical role in patrolling the Park's northern boundary.

Norman had a clear understanding of the importance of good road communications. Straight away existing roads were joined together to create a single viable route through the Park between north and south. Wherever possible, new roads were sited on high ground to minimise the damage done by the weather during the rainy season. To achieve this key objective, Norman needed the active cooperation of the Public Works Department which already had heavy machinery in the Park because of their work on the much-derided buildings at Ngoma Camp. Norman persuaded them to keep the equipment on site and use it for the construction of culverts and short bridges. This was made easier because Norman exercised his customary tact and refrained from joining the chorus of criticisms in relation to the Ngoma Camp buildings.

Norman had one major advantage in starting his new job. He was allowed to choose who he wanted to work with him. From the Game Department's European staff he chose two Afrikaners – Ernie Taljaard and Johnny Uys - and one of British descent – Barry Shenton. He chose senior African staff also, selecting Nelson Chilanga to be the chief game guard for the Park. Norman's choice of Afrikaners may seem surprising, given the difficulties he had encountered previously with Afrikaner poachers on the Copperbelt. However, having been born in Africa and experienced the world outside the security of the public service, Norman had a greater empathy with Afrikaners than some civil servants from Britain. He understood that many Afrikaners had a genuine – and informed – love of the natural world, combined with extraordinary hardiness.

Norman was fortunate in having Peter Morris already in post as game ranger at Kasempa. Morris had recently transferred from the police and was highly effective in maintaining anti-poaching patrols on the Park's northern boundary, even in the rainy season. Morris used the command-and-control approach favoured by most in the Game Department and the police: Norman seems to have been content that Morris should use tactics different from his own, especially when they produced good results. Morris's commitment to the Game Department was such that he persuaded his fiancée to postpone their planned honeymoon in Europe and substitute a fortnight in Kafue National Park. Norman and his colleagues made tourist accommodation available in a quiet spot for the newly-weds.

As Warden, Norman provided effective leadership. He achieved this by a mixture of evident competence (demonstrated by work accomplished) and by setting a good example. He worked hard and he worked long hours. In essence he rose with the sun and carried on working for most of the hours of daylight. His immediate subordinates followed his lead. In the first year Johnny Uys (pronounced 'Ace') remained close to the Park HQ at Ngoma, available to deal with visitors, contractors and unanticipated events. Ernie Taljaard seems to have concentrated on clerical work: he was later transferred to the Game Department's HQ to work as a clerk. The more experienced men – Norman and Barry Shenton – roamed around chasing up road-making and other construction work, keeping game guards focused on their anti-poaching duties, and maintaining good relations with local people and their chiefs. It was feasible to provide additional work for local people, especially in constructing and maintaining 'rondavels' (chalets or huts) for use by tourists. Norman understood that using readily available local materials to create cool, circular structures with thatched roofs was a low-cost approach that met the aesthetic requirements of visitors. It utilised the traditional craft skills of local people also. This did not prevent modern materials being used – mesh to keep out mosquitoes was incorporated in the structures, and some were given permanent foundations of concrete. As well as traditional circular houses at ground level, they built a tree house in the top of a large old baobab. This was modelled on the famous Treetops in Kenya.

Norman understood that to motivate African subordinates, and to get the best out of them, it was often wise to be patient and avoid direct questioning. He used heavy-handed disciplinary methods only as a last resort. In his book *Return to the Wild* he explained this empathetic approach in relation to a long-serving game guard called Chanamina.

> Any African enjoys telling a story and you must listen patiently and allow him to tell it his way; otherwise ... he is quite liable to give an account which he thinks might please the listener.... By eavesdropping whilst [Chanamina] recounted his adventures [to colleagues] ... I was able to get a fairly accurate version of his last patrol ...
>
> He hated patrolling in the rainy season but the Game Ranger, Bwana Morris, who had recently been transferred from the police, was strict and insisted that all game guards spent at least fifteen nights a month on patrol ... However, if he left his bicycle at Ndelemani's village twenty miles away, he could spend three or four days there and say in his report that he was investigating a poaching case ... the beer at Ndelemani's was good. Besides, Efeleni lived there and her husband had been away in the Copperbelt for over a year now. When he left Ndelemani's he could patrol the northern boundary ... along the Kabanga stream and come home via Chief Kasonso's village which was also noted for its good beer and hospitality.[58]

It was Chanamina who repaid Norman's trust and patience by bringing him two orphaned lion cubs. They would be known as Big Boy and Little

Boy and were the subject of Norman's first book. It is significant, also, that Norman made provision for a long-serving game guard to remain in employment even though he had a terminal illness and was not wholly fit for duty. The guard was posted to a quiet sector where he could cultivate his garden; he was required to carry out only short, easy patrols. This decision is likely to have had a positive impact on the way in which the game guards regarded their boss.

Barbara visited Kafue National Park at the end of the dry season in 1957. She listed animals and birds that she saw on her first day, when she joined Norman in the south. Her list consisted of: bushbuck, honey badger, kudu, a lioness with five cubs, wildebeest, zebra; and a bateleur eagle, bee-eaters, guinea fowl, lourie, pied kingfisher, purple roller, saddlebill storks, splendid starlings, wattled crane, weavers and vultures. Two days later they travelled north to the Busanga Plains and she listed: buffalo, duiker, eland, elephant, lechwe, mopani squirrel, rhino, roan antelope, warthog, waterbuck; and doves, ducks, geese, guinea fowl, plovers and storks. In addition, there was a boomslang snake which landed by her ankles in the footwell of the Land Rover. Any tourist visiting a Zambian national park in the 2020s would probably be overjoyed by an experience like this (possibly minus the snake). Barbara was not entirely pleased. She had hoped to be treated like a tourist. She may even have heard about Peter and Kate Morris's honeymoon and hoped for something similar – a comfortable bed, hot bath, good food, and relaxation on a veranda with a view. What she actually got was bruises from bumping at speed over rough ground in Norman's Land Rover (from which she fell out once), hurricane lamps for lighting, a cupful of hot water in a canvas basin to wash with, and burnt toast with smoky sausage for breakfast.

Barbara and Norman led separate lives from 1959 onwards. Mateyu, who had given Barbara such good service as a house servant, relocated to Lusaka. Norman's sister, Cicely, was living there and had been a civil servant for over a decade. At some point, Norman's mother joined her in Lusaka. Barbara published two highly successful books: *Not for me the Wilds* in 1963, and *Cherries on my Plate* in 1965. These became bestsellers in South Africa, and the first one was republished in the United States. In both books Barbara lambasted the British Empire, not for exploiting black people but for giving them unreasonable expectations, and for exploiting white civil servants. Norman came in for praise in terms of his wildlife expertise and strong criticism of his qualities as a husband. Although Norman published several books, he never retaliated. From the perspective of the author of this biography, Barbara's departure from Norman's life represents a great loss. Her books provide a mass of information that appears neither in official records, nor in Norman's own publications, and they do so in lively, beautifully written prose.

Kate Morris – a newly-wed in 1957 – published her memoirs in 2000. In them she referred to Barbara Carr's book *Not for me the Wilds*. Kate wrote:

> She was correct in every one of her accusations. The spartan amenities … persistent heat and dust … loneliness of frequent and lengthy absences … the competition … what chance did a woman possibly have when competing against the man's total and lasting obsession for … the 'Wilds'. What was not transcribed in that book, however, was of the joys and pleasures shared.

Big Boy and Little Boy

Norman acquired two male lion cubs shortly before Christmas 1957. He set out to bring them up as far as possible in the way they would have been reared in the wild if their mother had not died. He wrote that he tried 'to guard against the current sentimental tendency of crediting any animal with human reasoning powers'.[59] In fact, Norman avoided all forms of sentimentality. Crucially, he persuaded Johnny Uys to do the same. Whilst Norman was away from Ngoma, Johnny was a key figure in rearing the cubs. Another key figure was Norman's mastiff-mongrel bitch, Cindy, who led and dominated the cubs even after they had outgrown her: she died of trypanosomiasis whilst they were still young. Norman commented that the cubs '… were very inquisitive and any rapid movement would attract their attention and have to be investigated. But their favourite pastime was to stalk.'[60]

It rapidly became clear that Big Boy had an open and confident character which made him a natural favourite, whilst Little Boy was apt to be sulky, defiant, and destructive. As he learnt how to calm down Little Boy and to get the best out of him, so Norman became particularly fond of the junior cub. Norman reflected that this helped him to understand the behaviour of human mothers who develop special bonds with, and devote

80

particular care to, difficult children. In the dry season of 1958, the cubs were a great success with most visitors.

In his book *Return to the Wild* Norman gives a light-hearted account of an incident involving a new arrival from Britain who took a Land Rover out to explore the Park. The lions mistook the vehicle for Norman's Land Rover and attempted to get inside, causing the visitor great consternation. There was a more sombre aspect to having adolescent male lion cubs living near to human beings. Barbara took her own three children, plus their young cousin, to visit Ngoma in the school holidays in 1958. The cubs stalked the children repeatedly and occasionally knocked them to the ground. When Norman disregarded her anxieties, Barbara cut the holiday short and went home. A few months later, a young African girl who was visiting a relative at Ngoma was killed by Big Boy and Little Boy. She ran when she saw them, and they followed their instincts and ran after her. Big Boy knocked her down with a paw to the back of her neck and then they both attacked her on the ground. Norman was brought to court over this incident by the girl's father but acquitted.

Not only were Big Boy and Little Boy now too large, heavy and boisterous to remain at Ngoma, they were at risk also from Norman's snake collection. The snakes were kept partly for his own interest, partly for visitors' entertainment and partly as source of venom which was used in the production of serum. Big Boy was bitten by a puff adder inside Norman's reptile enclosure at Ngoma. So, by July 1959 the lions had been relocated to a remote area which was inside the park but distant from Ngoma camp.

By July 1960, the Kafue National Park was well established. There were ten rustic camps, of the kind that visitors liked, available during the dry season. The road network was good. The animal population was flourishing. Above all, relationships with indigenous people in and around the Park were excellent, and poaching had been reduced if not eliminated. His work in the National Park was finished and Norman moved to the place he loved best - the Luangwa Valley.

Chapter 8

Luangwa Valley

Warden of South Luangwa Game Reserve

Norman Carr took up a new post as warden of the South Luangwa Game Reserve in the middle of 1960. His situation was quite different from that which existed in 1957 when he arrived in the Kafue National Park. In his new job, he was short of money. As warden he had several game rangers to carry out the routines of patrolling in the Reserve and liaising with local chiefs. These were Bill Bullock as senior ranger and Lyn Birch and Peter Morris as rangers. Peter Morris had previously worked alongside Norman in the Kafue National Park, as explained in the previous chapter. Lyn Birch had served in the Royal Air Force's Bomber Command as a rear gunner and had been awarded the Distinguished Flying Cross. He was a strong man both physically and in outlook: he would later set up a safari lodge in Botswana. Norman had game guards to help him, too. Leading the game guards was Nelson Chilanga who moved from the Kafue National Park with Norman. Also present was Kalilombe who had been Norman's cook in the bush at Kafue and had first worked for him at Kasempa in 1944. Norman acknowledged that Kalilombe's culinary skills were limited but kept him on because he was likeable and dependable.

Norman had hardly any budget for new roads, culverts or pontoons. Although copper prices had begun to rise, government revenues continued to be depressed. Visitor numbers at the Kafue National Park and in the Luangwa Valley were still low, so locally-generated revenue was down, too. Fortunately, Eustace Poles had made a start on improving the infrastructure whilst he was the game ranger based at Mpika. His personal friendship with Len Gough in the Public Works Department may have helped in this endeavour. In 1955 Poles had installed a pontoon across the Luangwa River near its confluence with the Mupamadzi River, created sixty miles of dirt roads and set up two temporary bush camps: forty-seven visitors used these camps in the first year they were available. The pontoon was in the extreme north-east corner of the Reserve and close to the Munyamadzi Corridor for which Poles was responsible also. The access road to this area came in from the east, from Fort Jameson. The following year, Poles was given the support of a Public Works Department team with heavy machinery. This Luangwa Unit created 120 kilometres of roads that were intended to be permanent. These incorporated culverts and short concrete bridges, and had deep storm drains to carry off water in the rainy season. The Luangwa Unit started work at Chilongozi in the southern part of the Reserve where both the east and west banks of the river were inside its boundaries. Initially they constructed a road from Chilongozi along the east bank to Luamfwa Lagoon. Then, having found a good place for fording the river during the dry season, they made a road on the west bank which was intended to give visitors coming from - or via - Lusaka access to the heart of the Reserve. This road ran from Chilongozi, passing Mfuwe Lagoon (on the west bank) and Nsefu's Game Reserve (on the east bank), to Ntangi Lagoon where the Big Lagoon permanent rest camp was constructed. In 1958 Big Lagoon rest camp had 343 visitors and Chilongozi camp had 168. Unfortunately, when the river changed its course, a substantial portion of the road between Chilongozi and Mfuwe was lost.

Peter Hankin had a camp at Chibembe to the North East, close to Poles' pontoon. In the 1950s, when the Game Department had been obliged to halve the number of game rangers it employed, the task of escorting conducted hunting parties had been outsourced. Hankin had taken over the work, as a private contractor.

Norman set up his first camp on the eastern bank of the river, a short distance from Hankin's camp. Norman named his camp Kapani. This Kapani should not be confused with the Kapani Safari Lodge - which opened in the 1980s and at the time of writing (2023) is used as the HQ of Time and Tide Safaris. Today the permanent bridge over the Luangwa at Mfuwe stands about two kilometres upstream from the site of new Kapani. Norman chose a site in the shade of msikisi trees which, in August 1960, would have been in bloom and very fragrant. When he first put up his pole-and-thatch structures at Kapani there was almost nobody there. The absence of people was a particular attraction as he had the two adolescent lions with him – Big Boy and Little Boy. There was a settlement at Simoni's Village, but that was far enough away to minimise the risk of the lions killing another child – as they had done in the Kafue National Park.

Norman had two principal tasks as warden. Firstly, he was to carry out a census of the animal population. This involved driving and walking long distances across the Reserve and making estimates of the numbers of certain animals. Elephants, rhinos, hippos, giraffes, lions, hyenas, leopards, zebras, and antelopes were included in the survey. Rodents, birds, and other creatures were not enumerated. Secondly, Norman was to draw up a report on the future management of the whole Luangwa Valley, not just the South Luangwa Game Reserve, and make recommendations.

To understand what follows, it is necessary to know something of the topography and geography of the Valley. Norman's own words will serve very well for this purpose:

> The Luangwa Valley is part of a geological formation known as the Great Rift Valley … The Luangwa River runs … for almost four hundred miles until it joins up with the Zambezi … The Valley is almost two thousand feet lower than the surrounding plateau, and consequently much hotter. In the east there is no well-defined escarpment, but in the west there is an unbroken range extending for about two hundred miles. From the lip of this Muchingas Escarpment you can look eastward across a sea of tree-tops two thousand feet below, and on a clear day … you can pick up the gleam of the Luangwa River more than forty miles away.
>
> The vegetation changes as one descends … At first the country is fairly flat, well wooded and quite similar to the plateau. This then gives way to scrubland with stunted trees on small very steep hills … As one approaches the river the ground becomes flatter and the mopane tree becomes more common. This is the alluvial area … Mopane woodland varies enormously; in some sandy areas the trees are over sixty feet tall with a large straight bole; in clay areas the trees are much smaller and have a gnarled appearance. The riverine area has many assorted habitats and during the dry season abounds with life … The rainy season, however, presents a completely different face. In November … the tributaries, which are mere parched sandy river-beds in the dry season, come down in spate … The game disperses and the once-peaceful river appears in an entirely different guise – a

> turbulent, dark, muddy torrent … the alluvial area is flat and
> therefore usually waterlogged … there are two great plains on
> the west side of the Valley … The Chifungwe and Lunda plains
> extend for about 120 square miles and are covered by tall kasense
> grass … I once counted over seven hundred elephants browsing
> on the Chifungwe plain.[61]

The Chifungwe and Lunda plains are located on either side of the
Mupamadzi River in the far north of what is now the South Luangwa
National Park.

The special status of the area covered by the South Luangwa Game
Reserve had been recognised officially before the First World War. At a
time when Northern Rhodesia had two capitals – one in Livingstone for the
west and the other in Fort Jameson for the east – the area had been set aside.
This protected status was strengthened in the early 1920s when large-scale
copper mining was beginning to get underway. The company that owned
the great mines at Chingola and Kitwe carried out a geological survey of
almost the whole country, in search of other economic mineral deposits.
The Luangwa Valley was excluded from the survey: this protected the
area from development that might have had a detrimental impact on the
environment.

Norman submitted his report to the Game Department late in 1960.
His recommendations included a scheme for culling elephants, hippos, and
buffaloes: both as a way of generating food and income for local people,
and as a means for reducing overstocking inside the game reserves. His
investigation covered the whole Valley. Writing eight years later, Norman
referred to the Valley as 'The overcrowded ark' and summarised his report
as stating that:

> The human and animal populations outside the game reserves are
> an integral part of the ecology … [and] due to seasonal floods,
> lack of communications and the presence of tsetse fly, normal
> farming development was out of the question. The best use that
> could be made of the land was to turn its wildlife resources into
> cash revenue, to make wild animals pay.[62]

A conference to draw up a management plan for the whole Luangwa
Valley was held in Lusaka on 14 December 1960. Norman's report was
submitted to this conference and adopted as the basis of future policy.

However, the report was not acted upon immediately. Norman attributed this in part to the political situation: nationalist demands preoccupied the government. Dodds and Patton, who carried out similar work and produced a much longer report in 1968, attributed the failure to implement many of Norman's recommendations to a lack of skilled and professional staff and a high turnover rate amongst these senior staff. These explanations are not mutually exclusive: probably both were correct. In any event, the ideas Norman had articulated took root and influenced the Game Department and others for years to come.

In March 1961 Norman left the Game Department for the last time. Bill Bullock took over as acting warden and was confirmed in the job in 1963.

Return to the Wild

From his base at Kapani camp on the riverbank Norman had continued his work with his adopted lions, Big Boy and Little Boy. His primary objective was to train them so that they could be successfully released into the wild. At the same time, he was observing their behaviour and seeking to enhance zoological knowledge. He encouraged the lions to develop their hunting skills. He observed instinctive hunting behaviour in them and tried to hone this by leading the lions on bush walks that took them downwind of grazing herds. Initially they were clumsy, so he reduced their rations. Norman was careful to feed them with portions of identifiable animals, usually provided by Tsetse Control hunters. He did not give them chopped meat. From a young age they had stalked and pounced on Norman. Barbara had been concerned by the deep wounds that their claws inflicted on the stoical Norman. Now, as they were much stronger and bigger, he responded vigorously. 'If they … turn[ed] on me I used to beat them off with a stick which I always carried with me. This is the sort of treatment they would have received from their mother and, as a result, we understood each other perfectly. I was the boss lion.'[63]

Norman had written a book about his experiences bringing up Big Boy and Little Boy. In March 1961 during a visit to London he secured a contract with Collins for the publication of this – his first book. When the book appeared in 1962 as *Return to the Wild* it received favourable reviews. It was praised by Sir Julian Huxley, Director of the United Nations Educational, Scientific and Cultural Organisation, as making a genuine contribution to scientific knowledge. The book was reprinted twice because sales were good. A Readers Union edition was produced also. It might have been even more successful. But, by an odd coincidence, another book dealing with lion cubs rescued and brought up in the wild appeared almost simultaneously. This was *Born Free* by Joy Adamson. A film in which Joy was portrayed by Virginia McKenna as a wholesome and handsome British conservationist was successful: as a result, the book *Born Free* achieved huge sales. In fact, Joy was a neurotic, masochistic Austrian whose relationship with her husband George was close to toxic. Sir David Attenborough, the celebrated naturalist and broadcaster, visited the Adamsons whilst Elsa was still a cub. He wrote 'I had naively thought we would be able to film an idyll. Instead, violence lay beneath the surface wherever we looked.'[64]

A short film titled 'Return to the Wild' was made in 1962. The process of releasing Big Boy and Little Boy into the wild was delayed so that a government film unit could make the film. This was largely a matter of the Central African Film Unit filming Norman, Nelson, and the lions as they went about normal everyday activities. However, one 'extra' was added – a python that they called Charlie. The resulting film includes good footage of Norman. It was made using high quality 35mm colour film, so the wildlife sequences are attractive. However, the story of the lions growing up is unavoidably hampered by the lack of any film of them as cubs. Of course, cine filming was one of Norman's hobbies and he could have supplied footage, but this would have been amateur 8mm black and white film which the director, Anker Atkinson, did not regard as meeting his standards. 'Return to the wild' was released as a supporting 'B' film and generally shown in cinemas before the main feature.

The process of transporting the lions to their new home was a difficult one. Norman had chosen Mungwalala on the western bank of the Luangwa as the release point. Today this is within the boundaries of the North Luangwa National Park. A year had passed whilst the film was under discussion and in production. So Big Boy and Little Boy were now fully grown adults. Norman had to borrow a vehicle big enough to accommodate the lions and to transport them one at a time. The ninety miles journey took about eight hours. Little Boy was particularly ill at ease, '... at each lurch he staggered, growling, against the sides of the car or trampled on Nelson and myself.... He refused to calm down while the car was in motion. Bruised all over and completely exhausted, Nelson and I arrived .'[65]

A year after releasing the lions in North Luangwa Game Reserve, Norman went in search of them. He found them living in a pride as junior males with a dominant male and several females. Big Boy seemed to recognise Carr and came close to him, halting about fifty yards away. Little Boy ignored him and did not stop eating. Norman commented, 'The fact that both lions were apparently indifferent to me was a blow to my parental pride. But it was one I had half-expected. Sentimentality is an unwarranted luxury in the wilds.'[66]

Political Context

African nationalism had been given a boost in Northern Rhodesia, Southern Rhodesia, and Nyasaland in 1953 when the British Government created the Central African Federation joining the three territories together. Ordinary African people were concerned that more white settlers would come in and their land would be taken away. The Federation tried to counter this by proclaiming a policy of partnership between black and white people. Black Africans served in the Federal Parliament and one became a cabinet minister. Federation brought material prosperity, especially in Southern Rhodesia, and many improvements to government services. However, the distribution of wealth between black and white people remained unequal. Norman and Nelson became involved in a peripheral way in the Federation's attempts to portray itself as an interracial partnership when they visited London together. In practice, wildlife conservation and broadcasting were the only two areas of government in which partnership came close to being achieved.

By 1955 nationalist campaigning had returned to a low level. Things began to change rapidly in 1956 with the Suez crisis. Britain and France decided to use military force to regain control of the Suez Canal, but the action had to be abruptly abandoned when the United States government applied economic sanctions. The debacle at Suez gave nationalist leaders encouragement. Equally importantly, it led to a major change of policy in London and Paris. Following the Suez crisis, the Conservative government in London, acting in collaboration with the main opposition party – Labour – and the French government, decided on a policy of decolonisation. This was not debated in the House of Commons. There was no official announcement until February 1960. Of course, the governors and other senior officials in Britain's colonies were informed of the change immediately and knew that they must prepare for a rapid transfer of power.

Initially, African nationalists did not know that decolonisation was now Britain's policy. In Northern Rhodesia, as elsewhere, they were pushing against an open door. In elections held in October 1962 two parties competed for the nationalist vote. These were the African National Congress (ANC) led by Harry Nkumbula and the United National Independence Party (UNIP) led by Kenneth Kaunda. The ANC won seats in the South UNIP dominated everywhere else. Between them the ANC and UNIP had won two thirds of the votes and a majority on the Legislative Council. A form of internal self-government followed. British colonial officers continued to be responsible for the security services, finance, and external relations whilst most other departments had an African minister as their political head.

Another round of elections was scheduled for 1964 to elect the first parliament of an independent Zambia. In the run-up to the elections there was calm in the south and west of the country. David Attenborough, who was visiting at the time noted that the 'British Resident Commissioner in Barotseland ... who was held in great respect and admiration by the people he administered ... welcomed the coming independence of Zambia ... arranging for the coming of radical political change'.[67] In the north and east, including the Luangwa Valley, things were less settled. UNIP zealots, many of them young, were determined to challenge the authority of the government and, even more, to intimidate supporters of the ANC. In Lundazi District, covering the northern part of the Luangwa Valley, some schools were burnt down and there were minor disturbances, beginning in 1961. These had been easily countered by the district commissioner, Robin Short, with the aid of his district messengers (mostly unarmed retired soldiers) supported by game guards. The use of game guards in this way was unfortunate, as it made them a target when the situation became more inflamed.

During 1963 and 1964 order was maintained only with the help of the Police Special Branch in the form of experienced African inspectors. Nonetheless, beatings, burnings, and intimidation by UNIP's youth movement became widespread. Two game guards were murdered near Petauke. Members of UNIP's youth movement toured the Eastern Province, proclaiming the end of a wide range of rules, including the payment of taxes, and stating that all game could be shot at will. In 1963, Robin

Short was removed from Lundazi for being too energetic in maintaining public order. His replacement, James Mapoma, was beaten unconscious by an armed gang, and Senior Chief Mwase Lundazi, an honorary game ranger, was forced to flee. On 24 March 1964, Macdonald Lushinga, ANC Provincial Secretary, was beaten to death by UNIP supporters.

An unavoidably necessary aspect of the transfer of power to nationalists was the abandonment of old friends and supporters by the departing British. Amongst those abandoned was Norman Carr's collaborator Chief Nsefu. Robin Short wrote: 'Mercifully he died before the full extent of his abandonment ... became clear to him, and before he could be insulted by bands of political youths.'[68]

Into Business – Inventing Walking Safaris

Against a background of political turmoil and economic uncertainty, Norman decided to leave the public sector and go into business. In 1961, he set up a small safari business called Luangwa Safaris in partnership with Peter Hankin. Peter had a potentially lucrative contract with the Game Department to provide conducted (i.e., escorted) hunting safaris. However, the volume of business that he had attracted in the previous few years was not encouraging. In 1960 overall numbers of visitors in both the Luangwa Valley and Kafue National Park fell for the first time and visitor numbers remained depressed in 1961.

Peter Hankin had first become involved in the conducted hunting safaris scheme in 1956 when he had been given a contract as the 'White Hunter' (in official vocabulary 'Professional Hunter') guiding and advising the clients. At that point, the Game Department continued to administer the scheme and to collect fees. There was a second contractor, who provided catering services for the safaris. In 1956 there were twelve clients in total: all but one of them was from the United States. Each paid £600 for a two-weeks safari, plus licence fees for game shot. Each of them shot one elephant. In addition, they shot trophy specimens of the following species: buffalo, bushbuck, crocodile, hyena, impala, leopard, lion, puku, roan antelope, waterbuck, zebra, warthog, wild dog, and wildebeest. A total of 128 game animals were shot. Total revenue during the year, including licence fees, was £7,860. Half of the profits were paid into the accounts of chiefs in the Luangwa Valley, outside Nsefu and Luambe's areas (which received revenue under a separate scheme for Game Reserves). In 1958, when the Game Department had been subjected to major reductions in its budget, the whole conducted hunting safaris scheme had been outsourced to Peter Hankin.

Hankin's income from the conducted hunting safaris contract was about £100 for each client. In 1956 this amounted to £1,200. By 1961 the figure had fallen, not least because potential clients from the United States were apprehensive about possible political disturbances. Clearly the newly formed Luangwa Safaris could not provide a viable income for the two partners from escorted hunting alone. At this point, Norman invented an entirely new form of wildlife tourism - walking safaris. Before 1960, Northern Rhodesia had imitated services offered elsewhere. Wildlife tourism was much better established, and on a much larger scale, in South Africa and Kenya: providers in Northern Rhodesia looked to them for models. Now, with Norman at the helm, something quite new was being made available. Looking back on this twenty-five years later Norman wrote:

> When I first started safaris to earn a living, I had nostalgic memories of the foot tours which occupied much of my time as a game ranger ... To me the only way to experience the real spirit of Africa is on foot ... I thought I could simulate this experience by offering clients a safari, walking through the bush ... with a string of porters ... The idea was to find a nice shady tree under which to set up camp before moving on again next morning .... However, in practice this vision was quite impractical and as a commercial venture it was definitely not viable ... I compromised by building staging camps ...later these camps were furnished with beds and basic furniture.[69]

At the outset, Norman used a base camp about two miles from Old Kapani and on the opposite bank of the Luangwa. He called this Lion Camp. It had been built by the Game Department but, with visitor numbers falling, they had gladly agreed that Norman could use it. Lion Camp had simple buildings made from local materials but with some amenities that Norman did not regard as necessary at Kapani: these included doors and windows. Lion Camp could accommodate a maximum of six clients. In the first year of operation, Norman was assisted by Ron Kidson, a friend who farmed tobacco near Fort Jameson. The quality classification awarded to

Fort Jameson tobacco had been downgraded in the late 1950s and farmers' incomes had fallen. Ron was presumably glad to have a chance to earn some extra money. It was essential that Norman should have an assistant in this early phase, as he still had Big Boy and Little Boy to look after and was collaborating with the film crew in the making of 'Return to the Wild'. During this early phase, Norman regularly waded across the Luangwa River from **Old Kapani to Lion Camp** in the early morning and back again in the evening. Given the large crocodile population in the river, this was an extremely hazardous undertaking.

Lion Camp had an oxbow lagoon behind it which attracted large numbers of elephant. On the river frontage, hippo and crocodile were always in sight. Frequently there were buffalo and small antelopes to be seen. Norman's description of Lion Camp was: 'a more idyllic setting could not be found if you searched all over paradise'.[70] Unfortunately, Lion Camp was not big enough to accommodate the number of visitors required to make the walking safaris financially viable. In 1962 he relocated his base camp to Old Mfuwe which had a river frontage also and could accommodate twelve clients. Lion Camp was gradually undermined as the river changed its course and the last of the buildings there collapsed in 1976.

From the new base at Old Mfuwe Camp, and from subsequent base camps, the walking safaris went from strength to strength. Part of their charm was that Norman never lost his enthusiasm for them. Writing in the late 1960s he said: 'The companionship of a camp fire, the smell of mopane smoke, and the talk of shared adventures against a backdrop of African night noises is an atmosphere difficult to simulate, but once you have experienced it you are near to finding infinite contentment.'[71] Ten years later he was even more imbued with a sense of awe, writing '… there is one indefinable factor which to me is the most important … the spiritual quality of the wilderness – the serene sense of peacefulness it gives to a man's soul.'[72]

Norman published a description of a walking safari that took place late in the season in 1978/79. Starting out from Chibembe, the safari lasted for six days and made use of bush camps that had been built in April. The party consisted of six clients from the USA and the Netherlands. The clients had a briefing on the night prior to their departure. They carried their own binoculars and cameras, everything else was taken by porters. The party crossed the river using a pontoon barge, hauled by hand along a steel cable, presumably the one which had been installed by Eustace Poles in the mid-1950s. They were accompanied by an armed fundi, a former poacher whose skill and courage were essential in his role. The fundi always walked well in front of the clients, as a safety precaution. Norman describes the beauty and variety of the scenery and an impressive array of bird species spotted during the morning's unhurried walk to the first bush camp at Chikoko which they reached about 11:00 am. The clients had stopped every hour or so to talk about what they had seen, including elephants, hippos, warthogs, zebras, and various antelopes. At one of the rest stops, they had a tea break. Norman wrote: 'Meanwhile Kavinga … has a fire going and is brewing tea whilst we are overlooked by an excited family of vervet monkeys. This tea break on trail, when you are sitting down quietly alongside a stream or lagoon with half a dozen different species of animals in view, exemplifies the difference between … vehicle … or … on foot'.[73] During the middle of the day, the clients rested. Then there was a second, shorter, game viewing walk before dark. After a good meal most of the guests slept soundly. This pattern then continued with about nine or ten miles being covered each day. In essence, this walking safari of the late 1970s was not much different from the very first ones almost two decades earlier.

Luangwa Safaris received a major boost in 1962 when their contract for conducted hunting safaris was renewed for the period 1963-7. The new contract allowed them to have a maximum of thirty clients – an increase of fourteen. Unfortunately, news of political turmoil and violence caused concern amongst potential clients, especially in the USA, and made it difficult to fill all the thirty available bookings.

Chapter 9

Independence and Consolidation of a Safari Business, the early 1960s to the mid-1970s

Putting down Roots

In the early 1960s Norman Carr settled down in the Luangwa Valley, initially at Kapani Camp; then from 1962 at Mfuwe Camp and from 1964 at Mfuwe Lodge. These places were close together whereas previously, he had been rather nomadic. His early childhood had been spent on the coast of Mozambique. His education in Britain had occupied ten years and left him with an abiding dislike of commuting and large cities. Then he had become a junior clerk in the colonial civil service in Zomba before moving to Zambia. After war service he had moved repeatedly, serving in the Game Department in nearly a dozen different locations. On top of that, life had confronted him with some major challenges, including the early death of his father, the need to provide for his mother, a near-death encounter with a buffalo, separation from his wife and children, and bewilderingly rapid changes in the political sphere.

Two key aspects of Norman's philosophy of life enabled him to cope with the disappointments and challenges of life. Indeed, they made it possible for him to rise above life's problems and meet the world with a composed outlook. Firstly, he embraced the profound spiritual benefits that living in the Luangwa Valley provided. He was utterly sincere in his belief that the habitat, wild creatures, and changing seasons could cure souls troubled by urban living. So, by settling in the Luangwa Valley he was achieving a contentment that bureaucratic aggravations, extreme weather events, and other distractions might disturb but could not overcome. As a result, he became a natural - and highly effective - salesman for the safari company which he partly owned. Secondly, he devised the walking safari, which brought to a peak the benefits of living in close proximity to the natural world. He recognised that this could be achieved not only for clients but also for himself - by taking the time to really look at and appreciate the fullness of the earth, including insects, rodents, and other small creatures easily overlooked from a speeding vehicle.

Norman's commitment to Zambia and the Luangwa Valley was not absolute. He bought land beside Lake Malawi in the mid-1960s and built a cottage there over several years. He spent time at the Lake when the rainy season made life in the Valley unpleasant, and business commitments permitted his absence. In addition, he kept a bank account in Britain into which earnings from his publications were paid. The Zambian government had neither knowledge of, nor control over this account. These two steps meant that he had the option to leave if the need arose.

Independence

Zambia became independent on 24 October 1964, with Kenneth Kaunda as President and head of government. UNIP had a big majority in Parliament. Almost immediately the country became a de facto one-party state under emergency powers legislation. In 1973 the one-party state was fully established by law. For a year or two after 1964 there was a large element of continuity. The country retained a free enterprise economy, trade links to Southern Rhodesia and South Africa remained open, and the pound sterling remained in use. Importantly, levels of copper production increased, and copper prices rose due to demand from the United States, mainly on account of the escalating war in Vietnam. However, there was one aspect of policy that created problems from the outset. President Kaunda's government adopted price controls on agricultural products which impoverished the rural areas and started a rapid movement of people into the cities.

At an early stage, President Kaunda announced that white people were welcome to remain in Zambia as citizens, on the basis that they would earn the same wages and salaries as black Zambians. This was a clever use of an apparently 'colour blind' principle, like that used by the white mine workers' trade union in the 1940s and 1950s (see chapter 6 above). The result of President Kaunda's policy was that most white civil servants left the public service shortly after Independence. Unsurprisingly, most of the black Zambians who replaced them were inexperienced and poorly educated. Up to 1956 the British had anticipated that independence would not come until the early 21ˢᵗ century. Between 1957 and 1964 it had not been feasible to build up a sufficient cadre of suitably trained and experienced black public servants. In the mid-1960s, there was an influx of young white academics – many of them British – who were appointed to work as expatriate special advisers to Zambia's inexperienced cabinet ministers. This development was not much commented on as the special advisers were rarely seen in public.

Expatriate status was introduced for foreigners who had technical skills and advanced levels of education that black Zambians could not match. The usual expatriate contract was for two years. The great majority of white mine workers transferred to expatriate status, thereby becoming temporary guest workers. Most senior professional staff in the Game Department were on expatriate contracts by the mid-1960s. More numerous were the expatriate secondary school teachers who were recruited in large numbers in the 1960s. Virtually the whole staff of the new University of Zambia was recruited on the same basis. In the Game Department white personnel continued to dominate the senior levels of the organisation until the early 1970s. This was partly because few black Zambians were interested in a career that involved living outside Lusaka. Unfortunately, there was a rapid turnover of personnel amongst the Game Department's professional staff that led to a lack of continuity and disrupted planning. Zambianisation – the wholesale displacement of white staff on expatriate contracts – took place abruptly in 1972 and was preceded by an ill-mannered address to Chilanga-based staff by the minister, Sefelino Mulenga.

Large scale and expensive employment of expatriates was possible only because the Zambian government was receiving substantial revenues from the copper industry. By 1968 the government of Zambia was receiving 75% of the copper industry's profits in the form of income tax, special export tax and royalties. Much of this revenue was spent in attempting to diversify the country's economy, reduce dependence on metal exports and to promote development in geographically remote parts of Zambia. This policy was in accordance with election promises made by UNIP and was enthusiastically advocated by the expatriate special advisers in Lusaka. Factories producing batteries, bicycles, canned fruit, glass, and motor vehicles (assembled from imported parts) were set up in Mansa, Mbala, Kapiri Mposhi, Livingstone and Mwinilunga. Of these only the glass factory in Kapiri Mposhi was a success – partly because Zambians consume a lot of beer and therefore demand for bottles was and is high. Most of the new parastatal industries were costly failures.

Whereas expatriate teachers were sometimes willing to accept postings in remote areas, few expatriate or black Zambian engineers or technicians would work in places such as Mansa and Mwinilunga. This, combined with shortages of spare parts, lubricants, and other vital inputs meant that the parastatal industries had low productivity rates and had to charge high prices. Professor Andrew Roberts observed wryly that this might 'not work to the advantage of the Zambian consumer'.[74] In truth it represented a huge waste of scarce resources. John Mwanakatwe, a cabinet minister in Kaunda's first government, was more forthright than Roberts:

> the parastatals have not been successful … [they] are grossly over-staffed … productivity … is low … indiscipline … is rife … efforts of managers to discipline junior employees are met with displeasure … by the UNIP functionaries who … sponsored their employment.[75]

The parastatal industries programme was followed by large-scale nationalisation. The mining companies were partially nationalised with the government taking 51% of their shares. Similarly, the cement factory in Chilanga was taken into state ownership. A government-owned airline was created: Zambia Airways. Of direct concern to Norman Carr was the creation of the Zambia National Tourist Board and the National Hotels Corporation. Potentially, these threatened the future viability of his business.

In 1968 Zambia replaced the Pound Sterling with a new currency, the Kwacha (K). At the outset one Pound was worth two Kwacha and Zambia remained in the Sterling area. In 1971 Zambia left the Sterling area. This made it possible for the Bank of Zambia to impose foreign exchange controls and import licensing. Measures of this kind became necessary after the global oil price shock of 1973, when government revenues from the taxation of copper profits plummeted: in 1974 these were K339 million, in 1975 K59 million, in 1976 just K12 million, and in 1977 nil.

Consolidating a Safari Business

Luangwa Safaris flourished in the years immediately after independence. Norman Carr's commitment to stay in the Luangwa Valley was a significant factor in this success. His responsible attitude towards business administration was another key factor. Although Norman loved to spend time in the bush, he conscientiously set aside days to be devoted to correspondence, procurement, and accounts work in his office in Chipata. This continued until 1972 when the company was restructured, and the head office relocated to Lusaka. In his office work he was supported by Mrs Leach-Lewis, wife of the stipendiary magistrate. Even when he was in the bush, he often had a briefcase with him. His son-in-law, Vic Guhrs, has written about a dispute which occurred in the 1980s about an adopted warthog. Norman overcame bureaucratic objections from local representatives of the wildlife authorities, in part, by producing a file from the filing system maintained in his bush camp at Kapani, demonstrating that he had the matter fully documented.

Perhaps most important was his positive attitude towards African people and especially African colleagues. In 1965 he was one of the first safari operators to employ a person of colour as a professional hunter. This was Ishmail Osman, who recalls that Norman introduced him to Joe Joubert with the words: 'Meet my new Brown White Hunter', and that Norman addressed the issue of colour and trust straight away. '[Norman] … entrusted me with a new Ford Truck and money to buy provisions … However, Joe questioned NJC's immediate trust … Realising that Joe's question was based on my skin colour, Norman fumed and said it is time other races became more involved in this predominantly white profession.'[76] The first black Zambian apprentice professional hunter was appointed in 1971, and a mixed-race guide from Malawi joined Norman at Chibembe Camp a little later.

In his early years in business, Norman had good relations with the senior Game Department personnel who were responsible for the Luangwa Valley. Peter Morris, who had cooperated well with Norman when they both worked at Kafue National Park, became senior ranger in the South Luangwa Game Reserve. After Bill Bullock retired as warden, he was replaced by Johnny Uys, who had been one of Norman's 'right hand men' in the Kafue National Park. From 1966 or thereabouts, Philip Nel was the ranger with immediate responsibility within the Valley. Ian Manning remembers him working tirelessly to maintain the roads, keep the self-catering camps in order and to ensure that the game guards patrolled energetically. When expatriate staff were abruptly displaced in 1972, Johnny Uys reluctantly took up a new job with Southern Sun Hotels based in Wankie National Park in Rhodesia. (He was killed by an elephant the following year and his ashes were scattered in the South Luangwa National Park.)

Between 1965 and 1971 the Game Department was responsible for carrying into effect the policy of culling elephants. Norman had advocated this previously as a means of protecting the habitat from over-grazing, and shielding people outside the South Luangwa Game Reserve from the destruction of their crops by raiders. In one vital respect, however, this new culling programme differed from Norman's recommendations. He had advocated employing large numbers of local people to butcher the dead elephants, preserve the meat by air drying, then distribute the meat in the surrounding areas. Instead, the government of Zambia opted for a capital-intensive strategy that required big vehicles, a power generating plant and a blast freezer, so that the meat could be transported to the urban areas for consumption there.

There was one aspect of the political situation that was especially welcome. In September 1964, President Kaunda issued a special public appeal, urging all Zambians to cooperate in ending poaching and illegal hunting. This stated that many people had killed game unlawfully '… as a way of helping in the struggle for independence' and went on to argue that things had changed following Independence.[77] This appeal was followed by a successful amnesty on illegally-held ivory. In the Eastern Province (which included the Luangwa Valley) 2,079 tusks weighing 21,349 pounds were handed in. This suggests that in the years prior to independence subsistence poachers in the Luangwa Valley had shot over 1,000 elephants for their meat, and the tusks had been hidden away, just in case a chance to sell them should arise. This in turn indicates that commercial ivory poaching scarcely existed prior to Independence.

By 1966 all catered game-viewing camps in and around South Luangwa Game Reserve were being run by Luangwa Safaris Ltd. The Game Department continued to run some self-catering camps. The government had built some of the buildings the company used, and it provided some craftsmen to help: the company paid 15% of its total revenue to the government for these people and facilities. The range of services offered by Luangwa Safaris Ltd had broadened: vehicle safaris were now being provided, in addition to the walking safaris and escorted hunting safaris. During 1966 there was a total of almost 2,000 visitors on walking and/or vehicle safaris. They generated a total revenue of £14,233 of which £2,135 was paid to the government leaving the company with a gross revenue for the year of £12,098. To put this in context, a single Land Rover adapted for use in the bush and delivered to the Luangwa Valley cost about £1,000.

The escorted hunting safaris run mainly by Peter Hankin generated approximately £17,000 more. In 1966 a typical two-man safari lasted twenty-one days and cost the clients £1,627 (£813 each) plus £280 in licence fees. In that year, twenty-one hunters were catered for. Between them the hunters killed 362 animals including forty-three buffaloes, thirty-three elephants, nineteen hippos and five rhinos. All edible meat from the animals killed was either given to local people, or consumed in camp. The area awarded to Luangwa Safaris Ltd was 2,890 sq. miles and 'one of the best hunting areas in Africa'.[78] It included the east bank of the river, north of Nsefu's (except Luambe's), plus the Manyamadzi Corridor. Hunters who had been on safari with Luangwa Safaris Ltd in 1966 reported that: 'the very best standards were provided both in camp and in the hunt.'[79]

One implication of the pattern described above was that Peter Hankin spent most of the season out on safari with hunting clients. Ten two-man safaris of three weeks each would have occupied him for thirty weeks. So, Norman Carr had to oversee all the walking safaris, as well as the vehicle game viewing activities, whilst also liaising with the Luangwa Safaris Ltd office in Chipata over bookings, supplies, and so forth. This heavy workload, combined with the presence of Kalilombe, the cook who had been serving undercooked sausages and overcooked eggs to Norman since the 1940s, may help to explain why there were complaints about indifferent food in the camps that Norman oversaw.

Some of the tourists drove to the Luangwa Valley but most opted to fly in. Air services had been much improved in 1966 when Zambia Airways introduced a DC3 service three times per week from Lusaka, landing at the old Mfuwe airstrip inside the Reserve. The Dakota aircraft were basic, but they were reliable and that mattered to visitors. Unfortunately, currents of hot air rising from the Valley floor tended to create turbulence, and this had a dramatic effect on the Dakotas: some passengers referring to them as 'Vomit Comets'. After a few years they were replaced by Hawker Siddeley aircraft which carried more passengers. In 1972, South Luangwa Game Reserve became South Luangwa National Park. In 1975 a new airport, designed to accept international flights was opened at Masumba outside the National Park. Confusingly this new airport was named Mfuwe. Flights from Ndola on the Copperbelt had been introduced by 1978. A new permanent bridge at Mfuwe was opened at the same time as the airport. It was essential that Luangwa Safaris should have vehicles with which to collect visitors from both Mfuwe airstrip and Mfuwe airport. It made good business sense to utilise these same vehicles for game-viewing trips.

In 1968 David Patton from the United States Forest Service and Donald Dodds, a professor of wildlife management at Acadia University in Canada, wrote a report on wildlife and land use in the Luangwa Valley. They stated that in 1965 less than 5,000 visitors visited game-viewing areas in Zambia. This compared with 187,000 for Kenya and 225,000 for South Africa. Only 110 of the tourists visiting game-viewing areas in Zambia were foreign visitors, and of these just thirteen were from outside Africa – the great majority being South African or Rhodesian. Dodds and Patton hoped that the new international airport in Lusaka – opened in 1967 - would help to boost foreign visitor numbers.

Dodds and Patton referred coyly to Zambia having a relatively low population of salaried people capable of taking full advantage of Zambia's tourist areas. This was already changing by the time their report was published in 1968. The presence of large numbers of expatriate teachers and mine workers had a significant impact on the level and pattern of demand for safari services. Between the late 1960s and the mid-1970s, a lot of expatriate teachers travelled to South Luangwa, mainly to undertake vehicle safaris. In the mid-1970s this source of business declined steeply. When the government's revenues from copper dried up in 1976/77 the Ministry of Education failed to pay salaries and most expatriate teachers left the country. Something similar happened at the University of Zambia a year later.

Curiously, demand from expatriate mine workers rose against the same backdrop of economic decline. This was because the level of staff turnover rose dramatically. Experienced, long-serving professional and technical staff left in droves because of food shortages, restrictions on overseas remittances, and a deteriorating security situation. They were replaced with enthusiastic young people, mostly recruited from the British Isles, who revelled in levels of autonomy and responsibility that were not available to them at home. Many expected to work only one contract of two years, and aimed to visit both the Victoria Falls and the Luangwa Valley during that period. Thus, the expatriate workforce of the mining industry and their visiting relatives became a mainstay of Zambian tourism. In due course, visitor numbers were further swollen by overseas aid advisers.

Avoiding Nationalisation

When Dodds and Patton wrote their report on wildlife and land use in the Luangwa Valley in the late 1960s, they recommended that consideration should be given to the Zambia National Tourist Board (ZNTB) taking over complete control and management of camps in and around the Luangwa Valley. Alternatively, some element of private enterprise might be retained – possibly with private firms constructing their own camps. Neither Dodds nor Patton was a doctrinaire socialist: in recommending nationalisation they were aligning their report with the prevailing trends of Zambian politics and government. This idea - that all safari camps and activities should be brought together under a single authority was repeated in another United Nations report, written by another foreign adviser in 1973.[80]

It is remarkable that the government of Zambia opted for a mixture of state and private provision instead of choosing outright nationalisation of Luangwa Safaris Ltd and their small competitor Zambia Safaris Ltd, run by Ron Kidson. There are several factors that may help to explain this outcome. To begin with, there were no influential Zambians clamouring for nationalisation in the hope that it would provide them with a chance to take Norman Carr's or Peter Hankin's jobs. Work in the bush was anathema to most educated and ambitious Zambians. In addition, the turnover of Luangwa Safaris Ltd was quite modest – less than £30,000 per year. At a time when it was government policy to nationalise large firms, being small had advantages. Then there was the question of diversifying sources of foreign exchange. Wildlife tourism generated large forex earnings for Kenya and there were high hopes that Zambia might escape over-dependence on the mining industry by developing its tourist potential. By leaving private firms in business, the government enhanced the prospects of realising this goal.

It is likely that President Kaunda played a direct role in ensuring that a mixture of state and private provision prevailed in relation to wildlife tourism. John Hanks, who was conducting research on elephants' diets in the late 1960s, said of the president '… one of KK's attributes that stood him apart from all other African presidents of his time was a genuine interest in wildlife. His favourite spot in the bush was the Luangwa Valley …'[81] In the years immediately after Independence, the President stayed regularly in a simple two-storey structure known as The Mushroom which served also as a residence for the warden when he visited from Chipata. Although he presided over a government that was tarnished with nepotism, incompetence and gross inefficiency, President Kaunda was an essentially decent man. Zambia's second Auditor-General, who worked closely with him wrote that he was an 'honest, religious man who was … manipulated by others for their own ends'.[82] President Kaunda recognised that visiting statesmen / women were much more likely to be impressed by a visit to the Luangwa Valley than to an urban development project. So, he brought or sent them and relied on Norman Carr and his peers to act as safari guides. This pattern brought Norman in direct contact with the president and gave the latter an opportunity to gauge the depth of Norman's commitment and the breadth of his extraordinary knowledge. In due course a Presidential Lodge was built in the South Luangwa National Park at Kapiri Nkonde where President Kaunda could entertain guests or come to reflect and enjoy moments of peace.

A quarter of a century later, Norman Carr recalled one of the occasions in the 1960s when a visiting head of state requested a hunting safari.

> It was a shambles … we were assigned to the King of Nepal … It was agreed that the total number of guests would be limited to eleven … accompanying the royal party would be a very few select senior officials approved by State House … one of the ministers from Lusaka objected to Peter [Hankin] in the lead … called the Game Warden … to take over … the Warden in the lead … missed the turnoff … the missing King eventually … did turn up … not overly impressed … [we] were not prepared for the volunteers who insisted on accompanying [the hunting party] … the head security man … paramilitary with automatic rifles … police … photographers, making a round dozen in total … everyone had a great deal to talk about … after some days the only trophy was a mediocre warthog[83]

This kind of scene may explain why President Kaunda sometimes travelled in a comparatively small helicopter which could not possibly accommodate such a crowd. In due course, President Kaunda appointed Norman Carr as a Grand Officer of the Order of Distinguished Service. This was a well-deserved recognition of Norman's contribution and commitment to wildlife conservation. It reflected also, Kaunda's earnest desire that Zambia should be a multiracial and nonracial country. Following the death in 1967 of Sir Stewart Gore-Browne, who had been Zambia's most eminent white citizen, President Kaunda was especially eager to recognise and draw attention to white people who symbolised multiracial partnership. President Kaunda performed the opening ceremony at Norman's new base at Kapani Lodge in 1986. After he had been voted out of office, Dr Kaunda attended Norman Carr's memorial service in 1997 as a private citizen.

Peter Hankin

Norman Carr and his business partner Peter Hankin had been friends since the 1940s. According to Ian Manning who worked closely with Peter as a professional hunter, in the 1960s, the Hankin family had served the British Raj in India for generations. Peter's parents had moved to Chipata before the Second World War to take up tobacco farming. Like Norman, Peter had been a poacher before becoming a conservationist. They also had it in common that they had been married and their wives had become disenchanted with living in remote and uncomfortable places. Ian Manning describes Peter Hankin as being a gentleman. This was manifested in his loud, confident, voice and his use of starched white napkins (serviettes) even whilst on safari. Especially, Manning gives Hankin credit for ensuring that his mixed-race son, Professor John Hankin, received an excellent education and had a successful career as a mathematician. Manning wrote of Hankin:

> Peter told me that he had never had a client he liked. This says
> more about Peter than his clients ... Peter was a reserved and shy
> Englishman, though not one without a sense of humour, and I
> don't believe he ever had a close friend ... despite his so called
> dislike, Peter was the consummate professional, never letting his
> personal feelings cloud the excellence of that professionalism. His
> ethics were of the highest order, something I always admired.[84]

Following the visit of the King of Nepal, described above, Peter found that many civil servants and UNIP officials in Chipata and the Luangwa Valley now felt that they knew him. Accordingly, they pestered him for free hunting trips, free meat and 'presents' of money. He grew exasperated with this and left Zambia for Kenya where he worked as a safari guide for a few years. He returned to Zambia with the intention of setting up a luxury photographic safari business in the North Luangwa National Park but died before this plan could be carried into effect.

Peter Hankin was killed by a lioness in 1974. He was 56 years old. He had been camping on the banks of the Mwaleshi River is a remote part of the North Luangwa National Park. On the day of his death, he had been visiting Chipata. He had put his rifle into the gun safe at Chanjusi before leaving and when he returned the key-holder was away. So, he was unarmed when attacked. Norman wrote that this attack was a classic pattern of an old and injured lion turning man-eater. The lioness that killed Peter was old, thin, in poor condition and had three broken teeth. Norman wrote a tribute to Peter that is worth quoting in full:

> Peter was a friend with whom I shared many bush adventures. He was an exceptional person with great integrity. He was also one of the most knowledgeable field naturalists I ever knew, with an encyclopaedic knowledge of animals and their behaviour – a first rate ornithologist and botanist.[85]

Peter had started a newsletter sent out to clients through the post to keep them abreast of developments relating to the shooting safari business. Norman Carr continued this practice. Following Peter's death, Bryan Smith bought Peter's shares in Luangwa Safaris. He had been working as a professional hunter for the company. Ian Manning referred to Bryan's popularity with hunting clients, saying that he 'produced trophies like conjurers did rabbits'.[86] Bryan was a noted marksman and represented South Africa at clay pigeon shooting. Around 1972, Zambia Safaris, founded by Ron Kidson, and Luangwa Safaris, founded by Peter Hankin and Norman Carr, merged into a new re-capitalised company. The new managing director was Arnold Callens who had become the largest shareholder. Arnold was a bachelor from Belgium and noted for his erratic and excessively fast driving. The company's administrative centre was relocated from Chipata to Lusaka and Norman's role in office routine reduced accordingly.

From Game Reserve to National Park

The South Luangwa National Park was proclaimed in 1972. This heralded the coming of what a leading Zambian academic, Dr Orleans Mfune, has termed a 'fortress mentality' and an alienation of local people from conservation activities. It was symbolic of the change that game guards no longer wore shorts and broad-brimmed bush hats. Instead, they were issued with uniforms that were almost indistinguishable from those worn by the army. The new South Luangwa National Park incorporated the old South Luangwa Game Reserve and Chief Nsefu's Reserve. Seventeen other National Parks were created in 1972, including three more in the Luangwa Valley - North Luangwa National Park, Lukusuzi National Park, and Luambe National Park. Of course, the Kafue National Park remained in existence.

So far as wildlife conservation was concerned, the situation in the Luangwa Valley in 1972 was not ideal. Culling of elephants had ended in 1971. Those carrying out the culling had observed good practice. To avoid distress to individual animals, whole herds had been culled. The work had been undertaken using a separate network of roads in the park, to avoid upsetting visiting tourists. Nonetheless, there had been criticism from abroad and President Kaunda had been sensitive to this. Those responsible for carrying out the culling programme regarded their critics as ill-informed and sentimental. As Ian Manning expressed it: '... killing wildlife is to kill Bambi and Jumbo and to destroy their childhood ...'.[87] Logistical factors came into play also. Some elephants learnt from experience to avoid the area near to the blast freezing plant. So, it became necessary to cull animals far away from the processing plant and this involved transporting carcasses over long distances which in turn increased costs and reduced output. If the recommendations made in Norman Carr's 1960 report had been followed, the situation would have been easier to deal with: using local people and local skills would have allowed much greater flexibility.

The total number of animals culled between 1965 and 1971 had been modest: 337 buffaloes; 1,353 hippos; and 1,464 elephants. The figure for elephants represented just 1.5% of the total population. Nonetheless, it had served to slow population growth and to signal to local people that the authorities were in earnest about controlling crop damage. From 1972 onwards the elephant population increased dramatically. The habitat within the National Park was seriously damaged. Equally bad was the escalating level of crop raiding. Local villagers were alienated and, when commercial poaching got underway in the mid- to late-1970s, their sympathies were with the poachers rather than the game guards. Readers who are shocked that villagers should take this attitude might consider what Kenneth Bradley had written in his diary on 22 October 1938:

> Anyone who has travelled through uncontrolled elephant country and seen the devastated gardens on every side, or, later in the year, the starvation which results, will not think [crop protection measures] ...too severe.[88]

The wholesale creation of National Parks across Zambia coincided with a sudden and dramatic Zambianisation of the National Parks and Wildlife Service (NPWS). From this point onwards Norman Carr and his colleagues had to manage two sets of key relationships with people that they had previously not known, or had not known well.

Firstly, they had to try to manage a relationship with the NPWS Head Office in Chilanga. The senior officers in Chilanga were generally inclined to spend as much time in their offices as they possibly could. This meant they spent little time in the bush and sometimes seemed not to comprehend (nor even to care about) the realities of what was happening on the ground. Senior officials were often insecure and compensated for their anxieties by acting capriciously. The practice of safari camps' staff adopting orphaned wild animals provided a flashpoint for these tangled and tense relationships. On one occasion, a ranger based in the Valley asked Adrian Carr to adopt an orphaned elephant but was subsequently overruled by a senior officer in Chilanga who insisted on the orphan being released within the National Park borders in the certain knowledge that it would die there. Norman was well suited to this kind of work, even if he did not find it wholly agreeable. He was patient and polite on almost all occasions and had the ability to resort to anger only when he was sure this would produce the desired results without poisoning future relationships. Crucially, he recognised the difficulties which made Zambian civil servants' work challenging. Not least of these was the dramatic deterioration in public finances that followed the 1973 oil price rise and the evaporation of revenues from the copper mines.

Secondly, and simultaneously, Norman Carr and his colleagues had to work alongside a warden, rangers and game guards based in Chipata and the Valley. Generally, they had a good working relationship at local level. The NPWS staff in the Valley were often short of equipment, transport, and funds. So, they appreciated it when Norman Carr and his peers undertook work that the NPWS ought to have done. For instance, when safari company staff removed radio collars from the necks of adolescent lions: the collars having been put in place by a Japanese research team who then left when their research funds ran out. Similar work was undertaken for a lion with a snare around its neck. The comparatively relaxed state of relations locally is symbolised by the willingness of game guards to allow the Guhrs family to cycle within the national park during the off-season.

Maintaining good working relationships with senior NPWS staff may have been made more difficult by the presence of many white Zambians and former members of staff of the Northern Rhodesia Game Department (and their sons) on the professional staff of safari companies. These included Arthur and Patrick Ansell, the sons of Frank Ansell, a wildlife biologist in the old Game Department. Also present were the cousins Lester and Rolf Shenton (they were related to Barry Shenton who had been Norman's right-hand man in the Kafue National Park), Phil Berry, Cliff Bishop, Alistair Gallatly, and Doug Skinner. And there was Adrian Carr, Norman's son, who served his apprenticeship as a professional hunter in the Luangwa Valley. The characteristics of these men included courage and fortitude in the face of hardship and injury. Alistair Gallatly fought off a crocodile that attacked him in the Luangwa River and he was subsequently injured by a buffalo. Cliff Bishop was mauled whilst protecting a client from a lion and had a leg amputated. Doug Skinner had the experience of being hunted by hyenas when he was sick. Patrick Ansell was hurt by a snake. However, it should be acknowledged that Patrick's nickname in the Valley was 'malo wa ngozi' – the location of the accident. Collectively, these men enjoyed a high reputation amongst their clients. However, they were not natural diplomats. Part of Norman Carr's genius was that he could stand between the senior staff of the NPWS and the professional staff of safari companies and act as a trusted interpreter of each to the other.

Chapter 10

Staying on

Working Life and Family

Mfuwe Lodge was taken over by the Zambia National Tourist Board [ZNTB] around 1973 and Phil Berry moved in there as ZNTB's safari manager. Of necessity, Norman Carr relocated to a temporary base called Chibembe Camp in the north-east of the Park. His operations remained there for a couple of years and then moved again to Chibembe Lodge on the opposite bank of the river. Phil Berry joined Norman at Chibembe Lodge in 1976. He wrote later 'Norman was the grand old man of conservation in Zambia, a legend in his time, and I was delighted to have the opportunity of working with him'.[89] In the following year, Chinzombo camp was added as a 'green season' base for bird watchers and other clients who were willing to endure the humidity of the unhealthy months from December onwards.

Each year, between April and October, the pattern of Norman's daily life was an arduous one. When he was in camp, he generally got up well before dawn– and did not go to bed until 'lights out' at 10:00 pm when the generator was turned off. Radio calls to the company office in Lusaka would take place at pre-arranged times each day. During the day he dressed in shorts and a short-sleeved shirt. Whether in the bush or at base camp, the morning tea break was a cherished ritual. Most afternoons, after a shower, he changed into long trousers and a shirt with longer sleeves, often accompanied by a cravat. Vehicle safaris that departed in the late afternoon and returned after dark became a regular feature. Norman instituted a rule that if any vehicle was more than one hour overdue then rescue parties must set off without delay. He made a point of spending time with guests in the evening, talking about the most popular species such as lion and elephant, and answering clients' questions. Although he was asked the same questions many times over, he was invariably polite and patient. The film 'Return to the Wild' was shown frequently and Norman sat through a great many showings. He was, however, not tolerant of transistor radios or other devices that masked the sounds of the bush and he could be brusque in telling clients to turn off equipment of that nature.

Wilderness safaris – the walking safaris that made Norman's reputation – were sometimes accompanied by guides hired for the purpose. Nonetheless, Norman continued to play an active part. If he was not going out with a walking safari group, he would aim to provide them with a briefing on the evening before their departure and to spend time talking to them on their return. If he did go out with a group, he made a point of getting to know the clients individually. It was part of his skill that he found ways of praising clients for their fitness, or keen eyesight, or ornithological knowledge, or other attributes. To these compliments might be added positive comments about their countries of origin. This capacity for diplomacy combined with his expertise in relation to wildlife made Norman an ideal host.

Norman Carr was unusual in a number of ways. Not least of these was his long-term commitment to, and residence in, the Luangwa Valley. For much of the 1960s and 1970s he worked with a constantly shifting group of guides and professional hunters around him. Many of them worked for only a few seasons. As mentioned in the previous chapter, white Zambians formed a significant portion of this transient workforce. There were guides and professional hunters from other places too. One was an American, Peter Capstick, whom Norman recruited whilst visiting the USA: he stayed just one season. Another was Clive, a schoolteacher from the UK who worked as a guide during the long school holidays for several seasons. Ian Manning, whose book is referred to frequently in this study, came from South Africa and remained with Luangwa Safaris for four seasons, beginning in 1969, and then returned in 1979. One factor in the high turnover rate was that the main period of employment was from April to October. Most guides and professional hunters had to find other ways of earning a living between November and March. Some achieved this by farming in Zambia. Others went home to the UK.

The discomfort involved in living in the bush was a factor in preventing the forming of a settled, stable group of guides and professional hunters.

Even in the dry season, the roads throughout Zambia were poor and the distances to be covered were long. There were occasional shortages of food, and minor burglaries. More importantly, the available health facilities were primitive and a decision by President Kaunda to close private hospitals made matters worse. Indeed, those who lived and worked in the safari camps were frequently called on by nearby villagers for help with injuries and medical emergencies. The heat, especially in October, could be trying. Even the wildlife which attracted people to the Valley could become a source of irritation. Homes in the bush could attract bats, frogs, honey badgers, porcupines, scorpions, and a myriad of insects. Putsi flies laid eggs on damp towels, sheets and clothing left out of doors with distressing and painful consequences. Sleep might be disrupted by elephants and lions visiting camps during the night. And baboons liked to live near people because they had learnt this would reduce their vulnerability to leopards: this meant that baboon excrement was liberally distributed in the vicinity of the homes of those who lived in the bush. Norman dealt with these challenges with a mixture of philosophical indifference to comfort and diet, adaptations designed to minimise health risks and judicious outbursts of bad language and bad temper.

The Luangwa Valley did not provide an environment conducive to successful romance or lifelong marriages. Wise guides and professional hunters who planned to get married left the Valley and set up home in more settled places. Amongst them was Lester Shenton who took up farming when he married and who was replaced by his cousin Rolf. Norman was fortunate in having the affection and companionship of Chantelle Doyle, a British Airways stewardess who visited him in the Valley at frequent intervals.

When Norman's daughter, Pam, and her husband, Vic Guhrs, told Norman that they wanted to re-locate to the Valley his initial response was emphatically negative. Vic has recorded Norman as saying, 'Absolutely not. Life in the bush may seem very romantic to you now, even glamorous, but there's no career here for you …. There's no money in this, no security and no future. No. You stay in the city and build up a solid foundation for your lives'.[90] Gradually, Vic and Pam wore down Norman's opposition and in the mid-1970s they moved to Chibembe Lodge with their two small girls Tamara (then aged 3) and Miranda (aged 1). The Guhrs made a living as artists. Vic travelled regularly to the USA to sell his paintings at events mainly attended by people who hunted as a hobby. Pam's work included illustrations for her father's publications. The presence of his granddaughters brought an extra happiness into Norman's life. Although the girls suffered from bouts of malaria they flourished in the Valley and, following home schooling from their mother, attended a boarding school. Unlike Norman who had been parted from his parents for ten years, Tamara and Miranda were pupils at a British-style boarding school in Malawi and received regular visits from their parents. They were able, also, to return to the Valley during the main holidays.

Pam was not the only one of Norman's children to keep in touch. Judy had travelled overland to London with her father in the early 1960s. They drove there via countries that would later become hazardous as the process of decolonisation proceeded. Adrian joined his father in the Valley to train as a professional hunter. He later worked elsewhere in Africa. Eventually, Adrian became disenchanted with hunting because of declining ethical standards amongst clients. The established rule was that hunters should never leave a wounded animal to roam at will. To do so was to put local people at risk. The legislation that Norman helped write in the 1950s made it a legal requirement that hunters should follow wounded animals and kill them. By the 1980s, however, clients were increasingly reluctant to observe this practice being obsessed only with measuring trophies – horns, ivory et cetera. Adrian's view was confirmed by Ian Manning. As an honorary game ranger, Manning had a duty to uphold the law. When honorary rangers were first appointed in the 1950s, their primary duty was to prevent poaching by local villagers and disreputable mine workers. By the 1970s, however, Manning's experience was that many hunting clients objected to the limitations imposed by their licences being enforced.

Political and Economic Background

Ian Smith's Government in Rhodesia closed the border between Rhodesia and Zambia early in 1973. This disrupted trade and made some imported goods scarce. President Kaunda responded by closing the border on the Zambian side. The British government declared an oil embargo on Rhodesia and blockaded the port of Beira. As a result of the blockade and the border closure, Zambia's oil imports became unreliable and petrol was in short supply. In the same year OPEC, the cartel representing oil producing countries, substantially increased oil prices. So, in Zambia, fuel became both scarce and expensive.

When the United States was defeated in Vietnam in the mid-1970s, worldwide demand for copper fell. The price fell steeply and, as mentioned in the previous chapter, Zambian government revenues from copper dwindled to nothing before the end of the decade. President Kaunda was reluctant to take measures to bring public expenditure into line with revenue. So, he borrowed large sums. This did not resolve the underlying problems and he had to ask the International Monetary Fund (IMF) for help. The IMF made it a condition of lending that the public service and the parastatal industries should be subject to economy measures. This resulted in expenditure cuts focused on vehicles, buildings, consumable supplies, and every kind of maintenance. No one was made redundant from the bloated civil service or parastatal payroll. The effect was to leave huge numbers of public servants with no means of doing the jobs they were paid for. ZNTB staff responsible for promoting Zambia as a tourist destination overseas ran out of posters and brochures. In the Luangwa Valley and elsewhere, the NPWS struggled to carry out effective anti-poaching patrols because they had few functioning radios or vehicles. As the poachers began to arm themselves with automatic weapons the NPWS patrols – still equipped with Lee Enfield rifles – found themselves outgunned.

The IMF urged President Kaunda to reform the public services and reduce overall staff numbers. His response was to withdraw from IMF support mechanisms. An even deeper crisis followed, and the government of Zambia was eventually obliged to comply with the IMF's stipulations, albeit half-heartedly. For a time, the stringent application of exchange controls and import licensing was sufficient both to prevent inflation and to maintain the value of Zambia's currency, the Kwacha. By 1978 the Kwacha had risen in value by one third. But this could not last. The Zambian economy and public finances had unsustainable weaknesses. Many wealthy Asian businessmen concluded that there was no future for them in Zambia. They smuggled large quantities of Zambian banknotes out of the country and sold them to Swiss banks at a hugely discounted rate. The smuggled notes were then bought by representatives of the Chinese government and used to pay for goods and services whilst the railway from Dar es Salaam to Kapiri Mposhi was under construction. Meanwhile expatriate mine workers were selling their remittance rights to wealthy residents at rates which valued the Kwacha a long way below the official exchange rate. The cumulative effect was that exchange controls were rendered ineffective; inflation rose steeply and the value of the Kwacha plummeted. The Kwacha had been worth fifty pence (i.e., half of a British pound) in the 1960s. By 1978 this had risen to seventy-five pence. Then it fell, reaching thirty-two pence in July 1985. At the beginning of October 1985 it was worth sixteen pence and by the month's end only ten pence. In the 1990s, the Kwacha's value fell until it was worth less than one tenth of a penny. Interest rates on business loans rose steeply passing twenty-five per cent in November 1985 and approaching thirty per cent in the 1990s.

For much of the 1980s and into the early 1990s Zambia experienced negative economic growth. What wealth there was tended to be concentrated in and around Lusaka. Everywhere else, decline was evident. One simple example may help to illustrate this. At the Savoy Hotel in Ndola, which had once been the best hotel on the Copperbelt, the lifts and water heating system no longer worked and could not be repaired as neither the necessary spare parts nor the skilled technicians needed to carry out the work were available. When guests wanted to take a bath, hot water was carried up in buckets. For the poorest people in the site and service shanty towns the impact of stalled economic growth was dire. Unemployment rose, the death rate amongst children went up and illnesses associated with poor sanitation became rampant. In urban areas on the Copperbelt, where mosquito eradication had prevailed since the 1920s, malaria became a significant health issue.

Business

The safari companies operating in the Luangwa Valley were sheltered from the most severe aspects of Zambia's economic difficulties. They earned foreign exchange which the country desperately needed. So, they were given import licences and access to foreign exchange so they could purchase spare parts for vehicles, generators, communications equipment and even import some food items not available in Zambia.

In the late 1970s Zambia Safaris was restructured once more. Norman Carr was still a minority shareholder, but the main shareholder was now Leigh Clarke who had bought into the firm following Arnold Callens' death in car accident. According to Ian Manning, Clarke was attracted by the chance to earn foreign exchange quickly. As Manning put it:

> The company had been bought by a businessman, Leigh Clarke, a
> former client but now an individual captivated by the possibilities
> of making foreign exchange. It was now 'business' and 'deals' …
> there was no long term view; the unstable political and economic
> situation had made people unsure; rapid enrichment was the
> answer ….[91]

It was against this background that Norman Carr decided in 1979
to sell Chibembe Lodge and devote his time and energy to the Save the
Rhino campaign. Norman was explicit in saying that he had had enough
of running a hotel business. When Chibembe Lodge was sold, Phil Berry
moved to Chinzombo Camp and Robin Pope set up on his own in the Nsefu
Sector (where Norman and Chief Nsefu had pioneered wildlife tourism in
the 1940s).

Save the Rhino Campaign, 1979-81

The Save the Rhino Trust (SRT) campaign was in some ways the antithesis
of what Norman Carr believed in and stood for. The campaign focused on
a single species, whilst Norman had consistently argued that conservation
of the habitat and ecosystem should take priority over the protection of
individual species. Also, the campaign relied on coercive enforcement
strategies, whereas Norman had always advocated the importance of
engagement with local people. SRT relied on external funding and paid
only lip-service to the need to generate income for local people: it was
unsustainable for that reason. Nonetheless, Norman agreed to become a
leading participant. In fact, some people regarded him as the true founder
of SRT. He could, at least, argue that there was a significant benefit for the
habitat that could only be achieved by protecting rhinos: they are uniquely
capable of eating large quantities of thorn bush and by doing so they clear
extensive grazing lawns for antelopes.

During the 1970s the menace of poaching had become acute. Ian
Manning wrote that he had not seen a single poached rhino before 1973.
By 1979 the rhino population of the Luangwa Valley which had once
numbered 10,000 was facing extinction. It was no longer a matter of poor
villagers armed with muzzle-loading guns shooting animals for meat.

Dishonest businessmen saw an opportunity to get rich quick. Amongst them were dealers in illicit emeralds from Zaire and even Senegal. They could generate large profits on poached ivory. Rhino horns had the potential to deliver even greater returns. Politicians, magistrates and senior officials were bribed to obstruct and undermine efforts to control poaching. As a result, the sentences given to convicted poachers were minimal. Ian Manning recalled one case where a poacher was arrested immediately after killing an adult male rhino and admitted the offence; the magistrates' court fined him the equivalent of fifteen dollars and did not confiscate his rifle. Academic research on poaching, in which Phil Berry participated, concluded that lax enforcement by the courts was a factor in the failure of attempts to protect the rhino population of the Valley. Gangs – often composed of small-time criminals - were recruited in the densely populated settlements around the major cities and armed with automatic weapons. Villagers were recruited, too, on the basis that they were paid by the weight of the ivory and rhino horn delivered. To make matters worse, commercial poaching became a highly competitive activity with each gang or individual poacher striving to maximise the number of animals killed.

By 1979 the position of the rhinos was desperate. Numbers of surviving animals had fallen so low that the price of their horns had been driven up and this in turn created a frenzy amongst the poachers. Anti-poaching work was made more difficult by the attitudes of local people. They resented the failure of the NPWS to protect their crops from animals after the culling programme ended. Many villagers saw poachers as heroes, not villains.

Norman's work for SRT brought him into contact with HRH Prince Bernard of the Netherlands who, as International President of the World Wildlife Fund – later re-named World Wide Fund for Nature - (WWF), took a close interest in efforts to protect rhinos. HRH Prince Philip, Duke of Edinburgh, visited the Valley also, when he took over as President of the WWF. Prince Philip had been a high-profile spokesman for wildlife conservation long before green issues became fashionable, and many journalists had chosen to represent his speeches on the subject as diplomatic gaffes. In 1962 he had presciently criticised those who purchased rhino horn as an aphrodisiac. He shared Norman's belief that licensed hunting contributed to conservation by giving wildlife a measurable value.

The SRT campaign also brought Norman closer to David Shepherd the celebrated wildlife artist. They had known each other since 1964 and David was an impassioned conservationist. Like Norman's son-in-law, Vic Guhrs, David found creative inspiration in the Valley. David's daughter, Mandy, recalls her father and Norman as being:

> so very different – Dad like 'Tigger' ... angry, passionate, driven and desperate to achieve results by yesterday! Norman – quiet, unassuming, measured and an observer. But the warmth and deep respect and love that they had for each other was palpable .... Norman recognised that Dad could and would ... make a serious contribution and practical difference to conservation in Zambia .... Dad raised substantial funds for South Luangwa and ... [bought] a helicopter ...[92]

Phil Berry sometimes joined David and Norman to discuss wildlife conservation and although Norman was never domineering or dogmatic, he often had the last word.

Norman never lost his fundamental sympathy with local villagers who had become poachers because of the circumstances in which they found themselves. He wrote,

> I have a certain reluctant sympathy for the actual poacher ... it is the middle-man who ... manipulates these hunters who is the real criminal. I know one of the most notorious poachers who ... admits to killing more than a thousand elephants and several hundred rhinos. The most he ever received for his ivory was forty kwacha per kilo – less than the cost of tomatoes in any wayside market![93]

This empathy must have been evident to some of the poachers because many of them cooperated with the anti-poaching campaign after being arrested, often providing information that enabled vehicle-mounted patrols to swoop on poachers' camps.

By 1981, it was obvious that the SRT campaign had failed. There were estimated to be fewer than twenty rhinos left in the Valley. Norman decided that the time had come to move on. However, he did not sever his connections with the SRT campaign completely. One of his later contributions to the campaign was to write a guide to the wildlife of the Luangwa Valley. This was first published in 1987 and was sold to raise funds. It was still in print in the early 21st century and was recommended by the Lonely Planet handbook to Zambia published in 2002. Quitting day-to-day activities with the SRT campaign was not a reason to quit the Valley. The holocaust of poaching had scarcely had any impact on birds, buffaloes, cheetahs, crocodiles, giraffes, hippos, leopards, zebras or the many species of antelopes. In fact, the dramatic reduction in the elephant population had given the habitat a chance to recover from excessive overgrazing. Although much reduced, the elephant population was still large and beginning to show signs of resilience. Norman kept in touch with David Shepherd who remained a committed and passionate campaigner: David had the ear of President Kaunda and continued to be an influential spokesman for conservation. Of Norman, David wrote:

> … the only hope for survival of wildlife outside national parks now is by community involvement and its utilisation on a sustainable basis for the benefit of local people … this concept was formulated by WWF … [in the 1980s] … and enshrined in their world conservation strategy. However, Norman Carr was thinking along these lines thirty years earlier ….[94]

Freelance Guiding, 1981-86

The declining value of Norman's pension meant that it was essential for him to earn an income. The purchasing power of the pension had fallen gradually between 1960 and 1980: it had dropped to one tenth of its original level by the mid-1980s, and in the 1990s it became worthless.

Norman's next venture involved offering vehicle safaris in the South Luangwa National Park. He was approaching his 70th birthday and the days of long walking safaris were now behind him. He had three Land Cruisers and was assisted by Patrick Ansell and Lester Shenton. Guests were collected at dawn, so Norman, Patrick and Lester had to get up at 5:00 am. This business did not involve providing hotel facilities for clients. Norman was particularly glad to be rid of any responsibility for catering. As he explained to one mine worker from the Copperbelt whose complaints on that score had been especially vexing:

> I believe you have worked in Zambia for a number of years. So you must know there are shortages. That we sometimes struggle to get butter. Or flour. Or sugar. This camp [i.e. Chibembe Lodge] is rather a long way from anywhere. A day's drive from Lusaka.

> Three hours from the nearest shop or market. Fresh vegetables
> are particularly difficult ... We have no electricity for our fridges
> ....[95]

The clients for Norman's freelance guiding business stayed at Mfuwe Lodge - which Norman had run fifteen years earlier – whilst Norman, Patrick, Lester and the Guhrs family lived in a modest temporary camp, constructed of traditional building materials from the bush, which was located at the new Kapani. This Kapani is just three miles from Mfuwe and the journey over a tar road and a bridge was easy by comparison with the dirt roads and pontoon crossings of a previous generation.

By the 1980s backpackers and overlanders had become part of the visitor mix in the Luangwa Valley. Overlanders travelled in groups by truck. The backpackers caught local buses and/or hitched lifts. Flatdogs Camp near Mfuwe was built and operated by Jake da Motta specifically to cater for overlanders and backpackers. Yet a steady stream of backpackers made their way to Norman's camp in search of free accommodation. Norman was loath to deny hospitality to anybody and provided food, shelter and even free game drives to many of these people. Some of them were charming, good company and suitably appreciative. Others turned out to be freeloaders of an obnoxious kind. At Flatdogs Camp, Jake put up a sign addressed to that kind of person:

> Flatdogs Camp offers the most affordable accommodation in
> South Luangwa National Park. Quibbling about our prices makes
> you the biggest cheapskate in 9050 square kilometres.[96]

Norman's rejoicing at putting hotel administration behind him was short-lived. Mfuwe Lodge was now run by the National Hotels Corporation (NHC) and complaints from safari clients about the Lodge were frequent and persistent. At one level, the problem was quite simple: Mfuwe Lodge had been deprived of adequate funds for maintenance, and denied any fresh capital investment. So, it was tatty and run-down. Beyond that, there was a further problem. The management and staff of the NHC ran their properties according to what they thought guests ought to want, rather than asking the guests what they did want. The NHC imagined that guests wanted hotels to look as if they had been used as sets for early James Bond films. So, they furnished and equipped them accordingly. That many guests regarded this as incongruous in the bush did not occur to the NHC management. The NHC imagined that guests wanted waiters dressed in smart uniforms but did not appreciate that speed of service was infinitely more important to many of their guests. It was symptomatic of deeper issues that the NHC painted inventory numbers onto visible surfaces of the supposedly elegant chairs, tables, wardrobes et cetera in their hotels without realising that many of their guests regarded this as an indicator of bureaucracy at its worst. By 1985, the condition of Mfuwe Lodge had deteriorated so badly that Circuit Holdings, a subsidiary company of Zambia Consolidated Copper Mines, was brought in to renovate the buildings.

Vic Guhrs observed that Norman had:

> … become fed-up with the management at Mfuwe Lodge. His guests had been complaining – politely – about the sub-standard food, the inefficient service. When they leave, they enthuse about the outstanding wildlife, the fantastic game viewing. They praise Norman's knowledge …but they don't say anything complimentary about the food or accommodation.[97]

Before long, Norman began to think about creating a new, purpose-designed, lodge which would be built to last. Initially, he paced about Kapani drawing lines in the soil and making plans. Once the design and layout were clear in his head, Norman had the plan committed to paper. Then he started building. The new Kapani Lodge was constructed further back from the riverbank than Norman's previous safari camps, to avoid being undermined by changes in the river's course. This was successful: at the time of writing, the buildings are still standing. Central to the concept was a large chitenge – an open viewing area equipped with comfortable, casual chairs, and a bar – made with local stone, sturdy local timbers, and enough brick and concrete to make it an all-weather permanent structure. Accommodation was similarly robust and designed to exclude mosquitoes and other insects whilst allowing fresh air to circulate.

The construction of Kapani Lodge took several years. It consumed all the available capital and occupied as many of the skilled local building workforce as Norman could afford to pay. As a result, Norman, his colleagues, and the Guhrs family had to go on living in their 'temporary' quarters which their friends christened the 'Kapani Ruins' as they became increasingly dilapidated. Matters were made worse by a large troop of baboons which relocated into the trees around and above their quarters.

Kapani Lodge, 1986 onwards

Kapani Lodge was a resounding success. Its location, close to the Mfuwe Bridge, gave ready access to prime game viewing areas. The accommodation was well thought through and constructed to a high standard using locally sourced materials and craft skills to create an aesthetically pleasing variant of safari style. Catering became one of Kapani Lodge's key selling points, despite rather than because of, Norman Carr's attitudes.

Norman had intended that the food served at Kapani Lodge should be much the same as in previous camps. As the writer can testify from personal experience, this was a range of dishes that would have been familiar to anyone who had been educated in a fee-paying boys' school in the UK or who served in the Territorial Army prior to 1970. Fried sausages, bacon and egg were frequently on the menu. It was not unknown for a tinned luncheon meat to appear on the buffet at lunch time. When Norman hired Ginny Evans to be manageress at Kapani, she insisted on banishing tinned luncheon meat and raising the quality and range of dishes served. When she introduced four-course evening meals of a kind that might be found in the best restaurants in Cape Town or London, Norman objected to the cost. She refused to budge and showed him the visitors' book in which guests had written lavish praise for the food as well as the wildlife and the accommodation. In fact, Kapani now set a standard which other premier lodges had to match. Ginny and her husband Mark remained at Kapani for several years with Mark taking primary responsibility for the organisation of game viewing and Ginny looking after the lodge.

As business flourished at Kapani, Norman was able to add two satellite camps. One of these was a remote luxury camp especially well-suited to honeymoon couples. (Exercising his gentle sense of humour, Norman named this Nsolo Camp. Nsolo is the Chinyanja / Chichewa name for a bird, the Greater Honeyguide.) Belatedly, the accommodation for Norman, his colleagues and his family was improved also. The Guhrs built a substantial wooden home and commissioned good local furniture. Vic and Pam had studios in which to paint, and in due course a pottery shed was added for their daughter Tamara.

When Mark and Ginny Evans left, Nick and Jessica took over. At this point, Norman withdrew from day-to-day management responsibilities. He was now approaching 80 years old and needed a walking stick.

Nonetheless, he continued to spend time with guests, not least around the campfire in the evenings. Amongst these guests was Virginia McKenna, an actress whose outlook had been influenced by her starring role in 'Born Free' and who visited the Valley on behalf of the Zoo Check Campaign. Although Norman had reservations about it, a radio telephone link was installed at Kapani. His relations with Daudi Chimbali, warden of the South Luangwa National Park, were cordial. During the years immediately after the Zambianisation of the NPWS, relations had been strained. Now, when Daudi decided to introduce competency tests for guides providing game drives, Norman worked with him and prepared a training manual. Norman spent a certain amount of time during most days in his own personal open-sided shelter-cum-dining area: this became challenging for a spell when a hippo adopted the shelter as part of its territory and scent-marked it with dung on a regular basis. Even more alarming, although shorter-lived, was the episode when a pair of mating lions took over the communal kitchen at Kapani.

Norman continued to be an acute observer of the world around him: natural, political, and environmental. One January in the early 1990s, he wrote a description of the Luangwa Valley which is as evocative as anything ever written about the natural world:

> The atmosphere is clear, washed by the recent rains; the sand rivers which have been dormant most of the year have come to life dramatically with flash floods from the rain up on the escarpment; the Luangwa is full and is beginning to flood back into the ox-bow lagoons; there are clouds of butterflies, their colours as bright as jewels; frogs croak persistently throughout the night enjoying the flooded dambos; nurseries of impala lambs gambol joyously in the mopani glades; ground orchids and lilies are bursting into bloom; coucals and emerald-spotted doves are calling, and the constellation of Orion is rising in the evening sky.[98]

He could rejoice also over a momentous political change that took place in October 1991 as Zambia made a peaceful transition to multiparty democracy. When Dr Kenneth Kaunda accepted defeat, he became the first leader of a one-party African state to relinquish office without a coup or violence.

Norman was a sympathetic but clear-headed observer of wildlife conservation projects in the Valley that followed on from the SRT campaign. The most important was the Luangwa Integrated Resources Development Project [LIRDP] which was generously supported from Norwegian international development funds. It proclaimed a twin-track approach in which more effective enforcement measures would be integrated with initiatives to engage support amongst local villagers and deliver economic benefits to them. The enforcement measures lent themselves to monitoring and evaluation through the classic tools of project management – logical framework, enumeration of radios and vehicles delivered, output to purpose reviews, and so forth. Unfortunately, the community engagement initiatives did not readily align with these kinds of quantification. In its first year the LIRDP led to 186 arrests and the confiscation of sixty-two firearms. In the second year these figures had risen to 398 and 244, respectively. Norman understood that an increasingly heavy-handed enforcement campaign did not necessarily indicate success in winning the hearts and minds of villagers. Cynics could even regard the LIRDP as primarily delivering employment for well-educated Norwegians for whom jobs were in short supply at home. Norman expressed his view of the situation in these words:

> In the case of ... projects financed by outside donors ... a large percentage of the funds voted is absorbed into paying salaries and providing facilities for executive staff based at a remote urban headquarters and very little money gets to the grass roots.[99]

Norman Carr's preference was for small projects in which local people played an active role and from which they derived direct benefit. In his last years, he devoted much of his time to work of this kind. One of these projects involved the planting of gmelina tree seedlings. This is a rapidly growing tree that can be harvested for firewood and building poles within three years and which will regenerate when cut. It has an advantage over eucalyptus, which are equally good for poles, in that gmelina does not impoverish the soil. In the first instance, Norman worked with the headmaster of a local primary school: the pupils participated in the planting and their families reaped the rewards when the trees were ready for cropping.

Final Illness and Death

By 1997 Norman was becoming frail. He had serious medical problems with his kidneys, possibly linked to damage sustained when he had been gored by a buffalo forty years before. Specialists in Johannesburg recommended that he relocate there so that they could supervise appropriate treatment. This could add several years to his life, but he would never return to the bush. Alternatively, they could carry out a dangerous operation. Norman opted for the operation: it was not a success. He died on 1 April 1997. Norman's memorial service took place in the Luangwa Valley. Over 500 people attended. Amongst them was Dr Kenneth Kaunda, Zambia's first president.

After Norman's death, his daughter Judy moved to Zambia from South Africa to ensure that his estate was wound up properly and that his legacy was carried forward. She anticipated that these processes would take several months. She was still there and still engaged in community-based wildlife conservation at the time of her own death on 2nd December 2022.

Chapter 11

Writing

An Overview

In his writing, Norman Carr was first and foremost a populariser of science and wildlife conservation. He illustrated academic ideas with reference to daily experience in the bush and he added insights of his own. His works were written in a beautiful clear English which reflected his deep love of the habitat and creatures great and small, of Central Africa. His writing was enriched, and given a human appeal, by his concern for and interest in local people.

Norman's first publication was a short article that appeared in the *Northern Rhodesia Journal* in 1950. This provided information about opportunities for elephant hunting under the Game Department's Conducted Hunting Scheme. It is written in the impersonal, neutral prose of the kind in which official reports were written. As such, it stands in stark contrast with later and much livelier writings, published after he had ceased to be a civil servant.

Norman's second publication was his first, and most successful, book: *Return to the Wild*. This was written in the Luangwa Valley immediately after he had retired from the civil service and whilst his new walking safari business was a part-time occupation. Norman published this book with Collins and signed the contract with Billy Collins in London in 1961, after he and his daughter Judy had driven overland from Central Africa to Europe. Norman had originally titled his book 'Big Boy and Little Boy'. Billy persuaded him to change it. Norman established a good relationship with Billy Collins who was a great lover of African wildlife. In the 1960s, Collins published a wide range of other authors on wildlife in Africa including Joy Adamson, Jane Goodall, and Hugo van Lawick. Billy

Collins made several safaris to a range of countries. As his biographer, Adrian House, put it 'Billy Collins always relished the chance of seeing his authors and their subjects in their natural habitat'.[100] *Return to the Wild* was re-printed twice in 1962, was issued as a Readers' Union book in 1963, was published in a paperback edition by Fontana in 1964, and was one of three works included in an omnibus volume entitled *Three Great Animal Stories* in 1966. Collins went on to publish Norman's next two books.

Norman's next book was *The White Impala*, published in 1969. It is a curious book, consisting of twenty-one chapters of which the first ten are autobiographical and the next ten are focused primarily on habitat and wildlife management. The final chapter consists of a balance sheet of Norman's life and career. It is likely that the first, autobiographical, chapters were written whilst Norman was living in Johannesburg awaiting, and then recovering from, surgery on his back in 1956-7. He did not find it easy to pass time indoors in the Carrs' flat in Oxford Mansions and took writing materials to a park nearby. The second tranche of chapters was probably written mainly in Norman's new cottage in Malawi.

Norman bought land just south of Monkey Bay on the shores of Lake Malawi in the mid-1960s. The site was close to the home village of Mateyu who had worked for Norman's extended family for over thirty years. Mateyu had been a trusted servant in Norman's parents-in-law's home from the early 1930s. He then worked for Norman and Barbara, becoming the mainstay of Barbara's life as a young mother living alone in remote places, until she took her children to Johannesburg in the mid-1950s. Mateyu then moved to work for Norman's mother in Zomba and, up until her death, in Lusaka before relocating to Monkey Bay. Monkey Bay is a natural deep-water harbour and was the base for a regular service of steamers around the lake. Norman had a cottage built to his own design. This incorporated an upper floor in which he had a study from which visitors and family members were generally excluded. Here he could read and write undisturbed. There was also a shelter built of traditional materials. This was open at the front, with views over the lake, and provided a comfortable place to read and write if the study became stuffy. There was good fishing available if reading and writing lost their appeal. Norman made little use of the cottage between the months of April and November when he preferred to be (and business required him to be) in the Luangwa Valley. The lake shore was more comfortable than the Valley between December and March. Although they were at a similar altitude, there were pleasant breezes blowing off the lake that made the shore feel cooler whilst the Luangwa Valley baked between its escarpments. In addition, Malawi was a more settled country than Zambia. President Banda had imposed pass laws like those in South Africa (but without any element of racial discrimination) and thereby prevented the rapid urbanisation that was associated with crime and overcrowding in Zambia.

In the early to mid-1970s, Norman was preoccupied with the multiple challenges that resulted from expanding his safari business and relocating it from Mfuwe via temporary quarters to Chibembe Lodge. As a result, he did not have the leisure time required for writing. He returned to writing in the later 1970s, producing a short guide to the trees and shrubs of the Valley and his last full-length book for Collins.

The *Guide to the Trees and Shrubs of the Luangwa Valley* was published in 1978 as a fund-raising venture for, and by, the Wildlife Conservation Society of Zambia. It differs from many other books devoted to trees in that it reflects Norman's interest in, and knowledge of, the uses made by local people of the differing kinds of wood and fruits. He noted that: Mopane makes the best wood for campfires and will burn through the night; that Msimbiti or Leadwood is a very hard and dense wood, used for hoe handles; that Marula fruit can be used to brew alcohol; that Kapyiipyai, in addition to being the favourite food of giraffes in the Valley, has bark that can be utilised as a fish poison; that Msikizi is the best shade tree in the Valley ('This is the tree we chose when siting a new camp ....'[101]); and that Musanga or Winter Thorn can be used to make dug-out canoes.

Norman's next book, *The Valley of the Elephants, The Story of the Luangwa Valley and its Wildlife*, published in 1979, arguably represents the pinnacle of his written output. It is the work of a mature man who has thought deeply and read widely. As the title suggests, the challenge of managing a large elephant population to preserve the habitat is a major theme of the book. The first four chapters address the overarching topic and cover such themes as: the interdependence of animal species with each other and with differing types of vegetation; carnivores and their relationships with prey animals, including the role of predation in maintaining animal health in the wild; and other aspects of wildlife management. The bulk of the book consists of a series of descriptions of the Luangwa Valley in each month of the year. In these sections changes in temperature, rainfall and vegetation are related to breeding and birthing cycles and to animal distribution and diet and bird migration. The book concludes with a lyrical description of a walking safari which brings to life in the reader's imagination the experience of exploring the bush at a leisurely pace during the day, of convivial conversations in the evenings and of sleeping under the stars. In this account of a walking safari, the African staff who accompany the group - Wastikoti Njobvu, the armed fundi who walks in front of the party, and Kavinga the tea carrier – become real human beings with interesting stories to tell. Unsurprisingly, Norman refers to 'the spiritual quality of the wilderness – the serene sense of peace it gives to a man's soul.'[102]

In 1985 Norman wrote a pocket-sized *Guide to the Wildlife of the Luangwa Valley*. This was sponsored by BP Zambia and sold as a fundraising venture by the Save the Rhino Trust. It was a success. It was reprinted in a revised edition in 1987, and was recommended by Lonely Planet when they published their first guidebook to Zambia in 2002. The book consists mainly of brief accounts of mammal species found in the Valley detailing their height, weight, breeding, gestation, and longevity. There is a short section on reptiles and a check list of birds. The guide incorporates a two-page seasonal calendar which is essentially a heavily abbreviated version of the month-by-month text in Norman's previous book, *The Valley of the Elephants*. When Norman prepared a training manual for game guides in collaboration with Daudi Chimbali, warden of the SLNP, the *Guide to the Wildlife of the Luangwa Valley* presumably provided a convenient starting point.

Norman's business partner, Peter Hankin, had started a newsletter for clients and potential clients of hunting safaris. Following Peter's death in 1974, Norman continued the practice and widened the intended readership. In 1996, Norman published selected excerpts from newsletters sent out between 1987 and 1995. This *was Kakuli; A Story about Wild Animals, their Struggle to Survive and the People who live among them*. The title is Norman's nickname, given to him by villagers in the Luangwa Valley. As he explained, the term is used for older buffaloes 'singletons known as 'kakuli', maintain independence and do not associate with the larger breeding herds'.[103] *Kakuli* was not published by Collins. Billy Collins had died in 1976. Adrian House said of him that 'The African list that he founded … is still significant twenty years later'.[104] Sadly, when the company's accountants investigated, they found that Collins had been losing money on the African list. So, Norman published his last book with CBC publishers in Zimbabwe.

Although *Kakuli* appeared just one year before Norman's death, and does contain nostalgic references to his childhood in Chinde, it does not read like an old man's memoirs. He acknowledged that the day-to-day running of Kapani Lodge had had to be handed over to full-time managers, but characterised this as an opportunity rather than a loss. In the book he expressed optimism about the future and referred with pride to Zambia's peaceful transition from one-party rule to multiparty democracy, and to the complete safety in which his teenage granddaughters could travel around the Valley. Unlike the books published in 1968 and 1979, little - if any – of *Kakuli* was written in Norman's cottage beside Lake Malawi. In his last years he was no longer a regular resident there.

Reading and Scholarship

Norman read widely. As a young boy he was particularly fond of Rudyard Kipling's books. Looking back as an adult he remembered that in his teens he had been influenced by a range of writers who dealt with exploration, adventure and, above all, hunting. These included 'Karamoja' Bell, Commander Blunt, Sutherland, Lyell, Percival, and Frederick Courteney Selous. It is possible that during these formative years, Norman took Selous' positive attitude to African people as his own:

> In fact, to get on well with the natives of Africa, most of whom are very good-natured fellows and some of whom are among the bravest and most loyal men in the world, it is only necessary to be a 'gentleman' using that word in its true sense ....[105]

In the 1930s Norman's attention was focused on big game. He later regretted this, especially that he missed the opportunity to learn about vegetation and soils from the Colonial Office's first adviser on ecology, Colin Trapnell, who had been posted to Northern Rhodesia: 'I met him on several occasions … but in those days I was regrettably … not interested enough to try and absorb anything he might be able to teach me from his vast knowledge ....'[106]

It was only following his return from military service in 1943 that Norman became interested in wildlife in a much broader and more systematic way. Small mammals, as well as big game, became a matter of interest. Reptiles other than crocodiles joined his reading list. Before long, the whole food chain including insects, plants and trees fell within the scope of his reading. There was a natural tendency to focus on Southern and Central Africa, but this did not exclude other works from his library.He even read the pioneer naturalist Gilbert White's classic study *The Natural History and Antiquities of Selbourne* published in the eighteenth century. However, for much of his life, Norman was diffident about his knowledge of birds, writing 'I have a passing knowledge of the local birds but when it comes to the warblers and cisticolas, all drab brown and impossible to tell apart, I give up …'.[107] Latterly even birds became a subject of study and the onset of the rainy season provided excellent opportunities for bird observation. Much of his reading was supplemented, or prompted by, field observation.

Norman's thinking, reading and field observation were influenced by a course in biology and zoology for colonial officers that the Zoological Society of London provided and which he attended in 1953. The course gave him a more systematic and academic way of thinking. Although he read and thought deeply about a wide range of academic publications, he remained diffident about his own scholarship. This may be reflected in his attitude to the attribution of sources:

> … one accumulates a hotchpotch of knowledge in one's own particular field of interest, mostly an amalgam of facts from personal observations mixed in with other people's findings … it is difficult to separate one's own original ideas from those of others. I personally find it tedious when reading … to be interrupted along every line by references to previous learned authors who have contributed to these opinions. So if I have missed out giving credit I offer my apologies. I am told if I steal one person's ideas I am guilty of plagiarism but if I quote from more than one source it is called research![108]

One factor in Norman's curious lack of confidence in his own standing as a scholar is his acute awareness of his own lack of formal higher education. Unlike many of the men of the Colonial Administrative Service, alongside whom he had served in Zomba in the1930s, he had not been to

Oxford or Cambridge universities. Nor had he attended one of the more prestigious boys' boarding schools like Sedbergh or Fettes. This distinction was about class as well as education. Its importance had been made clear to Norman whilst he was in Nyasaland: his place in the official order of precedence was at the bottom; at any dinner party he was seated on the outer fringes; even in the government's cricket team, less capable men had to bat before him because of their higher status. Of course, having held the King's Commission in the army did raise his standing in official eyes after 1943, but lessons learnt early in his working life remained with him.

Although Norman did not always, or systematically, acknowledge authors whose work had influenced him, it is instructive simply to list those he does name, to illustrate the range of his reading: W F H (Frank) Ansell, Robert Ardrey, Richard Bell, Phil Berry, Graeme Caughley, Raymond Dart, Eliot Howard, Hans Kruuk, J S B Leakey, David Livingstone, Eugene Marais, Cynthia Moss, Katharine Boynton Payne, George Schaller, Shirley Strum and Peter Tolson.

Norman read for light entertainment as well as in search of knowledge. He had a particular liking for crime novels or whodunnits. These were a mainstay of his reading during the busiest times of the year when the routine chores of running a safari company occupied much of his time and a little escapism helped him to relax.

Ideas

Norman Carr's fundamental ideas about wildlife and conservation were fully formed by the time his first book, *Return to the Wild*, was written in 1960-1. They had been formulated, adapted, and developed between 1943 and 1960 on the basis of observation, reading and analytical thinking. The report that he wrote on the future management of the Luangwa Valley in 1960 (described in chapter 8 above) served to crystalise Norman's ideas: in essence, they remained the same from that point on. However, he did not ignore changes in the external political and economic environment and he actively assimilated new research.

The bedrock of Norman's views was that the management of the habitat should take priority over concerns in relation to specific species. He was convinced that the management of wildlife reserves as sanctuaries had led to unsustainable population growth - in the case of the Luangwa Valley in the elephant and hippo populations - and that this threatened to bring catastrophic consequences. He elaborated on this idea in his second book, *The White Impala* and it is worth quoting that at length:

> The end product of overcrowding is obvious to those on the spot … as the numbers of animals increase and more of the available food is used up, the animals begin to lose condition …. One of the manifestations of over-population happens when the land loses its top-soil … rain water then runs off, forming gullies, and progressive erosion sets in. Once the habitat is ruined … and erosion takes place, nature needs ten thousand years to replace … soil … it is much more important to conserve the habitat than to protect the animals.[109]

He reinforced his argument by referring to historical experience:

> Towards the end of the 1890s, the wild animal population cycle in Africa seemed to reach a peak. Habitats became degraded, animals lost condition and their natural resistance was reduced … The rinderpest epidemic … swept southward … leaving millions of dead animals in its wake … It has taken more than sixty years for the wild animals to build up again.[110]

Norman made a point of acknowledging alternative theories and proposals for policy that differed from, even contradicted, his own. He did so with characteristic courtesy and good manners. In advocating culling as the optimal solution of overpopulation he referred to the competing 'stable life cycle' theory which emphasises the ability of the natural world to self-regulate. Proponents of the 'stable life cycle' base their theory on the observation that fertility levels, especially in mammals, drop significantly in response to shortages of food and other adverse environmental factors. Thus, a reduced birth rate compensates for depletion of the habitat and thereby a new sustainable equilibrium may be achieved. In response, Norman argued that the unusually long lifespan of elephants renders this approach impracticable. Young elephants born last year will go on damaging a depleted habitat for the whole of their fifty to sixty year lives and this alone guarantees an existential crisis when overconsumption of vegetation is already at critical levels. On this basis, he argued in favour of systematic culling of surplus animal populations. Ironically, the debate was settled by a sudden growth in commercial poaching. This resulted in a massive drop in the elephant population of the Luangwa Valley. In the mid-1980s Norman reckoned the number of elephants had dropped from 100,000 to 30,000 and that even the latter number might be too big to be sustainable. Ten years later, he accepted that the stabilisation of the population at approximately 15,000 animals made it unnecessary to resume culling. In Norman's view, the real tragedy of industrial-scale poaching was the extermination of the rhino population. Rhinoceroses, far from threatening the habitat, had modified the riverine areas beneficially to create grazing lawns for antelopes.

At the heart of Norman's thinking was the interdependence of living things, including trees and other forms of vegetation. He knew from observation that by the 1970s the dominant species of tree in the Luangwa Valley, the mopane, was being devastated by overconsumption by elephants. He quotes Caughley as stating that four per cent of mature mopane trees were being felled by elephants each year by the 1970s. To this Norman added an estimate of his own – that if trees killed by ring-barking were taken into account then the rate of loss was eight per cent per year. This was clearly unsustainable. In addition, trees of the kigelia / combretum type were being modified by removal of branches at a rate well in excess of their annual regrowth rate. As Norman's personal knowledge of the Valley stretched back over half a century, he was in a position to add that baobabs had not become part of elephants' diet until the 1950s and that population growth seemed to provide the best explanation for the dramatic levels of damage inflicted.

The role of predators was another topic in relation to the interdependence of living things that interested Norman. He was certain that they played a key role in maintaining health amongst prey animals. By killing sick and old animals, predators ensure that only those in good condition have an opportunity to breed. He illustrated this argument by referring to Lochinvar National Park on the Kafue Flats. All prey animals there had been eliminated and, as a result, the entire population of lechwe was afflicted with disease. Beyond this definite belief in the benefit of predation for prey animals' health, Norman adopted a nuanced and open-minded attitude towards the relationship between predators and prey animals. He acknowledged that the availability of food and other habitat factors were likely to be the main determinants of the size of prey animals' herds.

Beyond that basic observation, he kept an open mind on the question whether predators control prey animals' numbers or the other way around. Norman considered separately each of the main species of predators present in the Valley, recognising that the predator – prey relationship might vary between lions, hyenas, wild dogs, leopards, and crocodiles. He noted, that lesser predators – serval, genet, mongoose, snakes, and birds of prey - had a role in relation to small prey animals, insects, and birds. The latter appeared to be plentiful but there was insufficient empirical evidence available to make worthwhile generalisations possible.

Norman was clear that for wildlife to have a viable future it was essential that wild animals and wild habitats should generate tangible benefits for humankind. He thought this was a universal truth, but his main focus was on Sub-Saharan Africa with its poverty and rapid population growth. Here, he argued, neither sentimentality nor free-access leisure pursuits could provide an adequate basis for sustainably setting aside large areas of land. In the case of Zambia one eighth of the country lay in national parks and this pattern could only continue if material benefits were seen to come from it. Norman's son-in-law, Vic Guhrs illustrated the challenge by attempting to see things from the perspective of the urban poor who live in:

> abysmally squalid shanty towns … sewage runs between the small
> houses in open drains, a fertile conduit for dysentery … there is
> the all-pervading, stifling haze from charcoal fires …. The AIDS
> epidemic is adding fuel to the fire of poverty, unemployment and
> misery ….
> But [foreigners] want wildlife.[111]

Given Norman Carr's concern with revenue generation, and his previous experience, it is no surprise that he was a staunch supporter of licensed big game hunting. Hunters, whether wealthy residents of an African country or foreigners, generated income for central government in the form of licence fees. They supported employment for local people, most importantly in the remote rural areas where national parks are located and where paid employment was often scarce. The meat from their kills was not wasted: whatever was not consumed in camp was given to local villagers. And many of the animal species shot – elephants, buffaloes, hippos and crocodiles - were present in superabundance. Norman knew that some people disapproved of hunting on principle, including his own granddaughters, and he no longer felt the extreme excitement that hunting had evoked in him as a young man. Nonetheless, he made the case for hunting not only in terms of benefit for people in poor African countries but on the basis of evolutionary principle also. Hunting, he believed, was essentially like exploration, mountain climbing, and a range of challenging pursuits including innovation in music and art. He argued:

> that early man was a hunter, that contemporary man has inherited this instinct, that instincts ... are ineradicable even though civilisation compels us to inhibit them, that the will to dominate ... often finds expression in adventurous pursuits, particularly hunting ... we may try to moralise about it [but] we must face the fact that instincts can be successfully channelled but not denied ... we belong to the order of nature, and hunting is of that order ... this is not to insist we should all do it ... but that we should understand it ....[112]

Norman's advocacy for hunting is out of step with dominant ideas in the 21st century western world. It may even make him appear antediluvian. His innovative ideas in relation to community-based wildlife conservation, on the other hand, make him seem far-sighted and progressive.

Following Zambia's independence, Norman Carr believed that two main direct benefits from wildlife ought to be evident to local people: paid employment, and protein in the form of meat. The form of culling that he advocated in the 1960s would have delivered these abundantly. He was conscious also of the need to avoid disbenefits, principally crop damage by wild animals raiding villagers' gardens. In addition, he supported efforts to work with teachers to introduce the basic principles of conservation to school pupils. His motivation was not just transactional. He regarded local villagers as fundamentally decent, good people and wanted to help them for their own sake, not just as a means to achieving the conservation of wildlife.

His earlier concept of community-based wildlife conservation had involved generating income for local chiefs' treasuries. In this iteration, community-based meant that devolved local administrations received from tourists' money that could be used to fund clinics, schools, roads and bridges, producer cooperatives, and even bursaries for exceptional pupils to attend secondary school. Norman understood that chiefs who adopted the conservation of wildlife as a viable source of revenue would also enforce the licensing of firearms and of dogs, thereby generating even more revenue whilst reducing poaching. Chief Nsefu's success in the 1950s in adopting this strategy encouraged other chiefs to follow suit, both in the Luangwa Valley and elsewhere in the country.

Following Independence there was a fundamental shift of power to the centre. Chiefs continued to exist, but their autonomy was constrained, and their remit reduced. In the 21st century, good community-based wildlife conservation projects continue to work with local chiefs, but the tangible benefits to local people are no longer as self-evident as they were prior to the widespread declaration of national parks across Zambia in 1972.

Business Aspects

Norman earned a significant amount of money from three of his books. The records of William Collins show that he received £1,575 in advances and royalties on *Return to the Wild* (this figure does not include royalties on the paperback edition), £1,445 in advances and royalties for *The White Impala*, and £1,500 in advances for *The Valley of the Elephants*. These sums can be contrasted with the £500 which Norman received annually as a pension in the mid-1960s. Unfortunately, no figures are available for royalties on *The Valley of the Elephants* or in respect of his other publications. In any case, he would not have received royalties for the short publication on trees, or the pocket-sized guide to wildlife, as those were published as fundraisers for the WCSZ and SRT respectively. When Norman signed his contract with William Collins in 1961, his royalties were to be paid into his Barclays Bank account in Lusaka. By 1969 this had been changed and his earnings were being paid into an account with Barclays Bank in London. This meant that his earnings from publications did not fall within the scope of Zambia's exchange controls and were exempt from income tax. Norman's last book represents a classic pattern of behaviour amongst authors: gathering texts that had been written for another purpose and making a book out of them. It can be a good way to generate income but that was probably not Norman's prime intention. In fact, CBC Publishing had to obtain a donation from Barclays Bank Zambia towards the cost of publication which suggests that only modest sales were anticipated.

In addition to providing him with an additional source of income, Norman's publications served a second purpose. They gave him an opportunity to advertise. In some respects, this was a straightforward matter. For example, in the *Guide to the wildlife of the Luangwa Valley*, Norman's name and his address at Kapani Lodge appear in the introduction, and the details of the travel agent in Lusaka through whom bookings could be made are given on the last page. There are more subtle variants of advertising taking place also. The many accounts of exciting episodes and unusual challenges serve to whet the appetite of the potential client. In addition, the evocative descriptions of cool early mornings, well-earned tea breaks, the scent of newly opened flowers, the beauty of fresh foliage, the glories of an African sunset, the companionship of the campfire, and the spiritual sensations evoked by sleeping under the stars, all encourage those who have been on safari before to return. Introductory texts by the Earl of Dalhousie (1962), Prince Bernhard of the Netherlands (1969), President Kaunda (1985) and David Shepherd (1996) all served to emphasise Norman's status as the foremost expert on wildlife in Zambia. Lord Dalhousie set the pattern at the outset when he described Norman's courage in going unarmed and added, 'Charming and modest, [Norman] has that deep understanding, almost a philosophy, with which Nature endows only a select few.'[113] More than thirty years later, David Shepherd added 'Norman is surely more qualified than almost anyone else to discuss the habits and behaviour of the animals he knows so well …'.[114]

Significant Silences

There are several topics on which Norman chose to remain silent in his writing. Like most people he had constructed a narrative of his life's experiences: unlike most people he wrote his down. One motivation seems to have been the promotion of his business. His success in attracting clients to his safaris rested on maintaining an image and avoiding subjects that might disturb or deter potential customers.

Norman had received a good education which was designed to equip him for a working life in commerce. However, having an expertise in bookkeeping techniques and a knowledge of shorthand did not align easily with his image as wildlife expert and bush man. So, his publications never devoted space to details of a crucial period of his life between the ages of 7 and 17. Similarly, another formative eight years of his life, as a clerical officer in the Colonial Civil Service, is almost entirely absent from his books. The nearest he got to acknowledging this phase of his life was the words 'I was compelled to settle down and take up a regular job with the Nyasaland Government' but he added no details of what he did or with whom he worked.[115] These omissions are significant. The focus and content of his schooling was a factor in the success of his safari business ventures after 1960. Similarly, his time in the Secretariat in Zomba contributed to his successes in the Game Department of neighbouring Northern Rhodesia. Not least, having an insight into the internal workings of the Colonial Civil Service helped him to ensure that Chief Nsefu's groundbreaking wildlife reserve came to fruition. His accomplishments as a cricketer, in London and Nyasaland, vanish from Norman's narrative of his life as a necessary consequence of avoiding any mention of his schooling and clerical career.

Norman chose not to say that he had been discharged from the King's African Rifles, along with many other officers from agricultural backgrounds, in 1943. What he wrote about his military service is vague to the point of being misleading. He accurately stated that he had been a company commander. The rank of captain is normally given to company commanders and Norman allowed people to assume he had been a captain. No doubt, if he had remained in the army after completing his tactical training course at Gilgil then he would have been promoted, but he never was. This may be a minor and even innocent deception, but it had the consequence that his service with the Game Department in Kasempa between 1943 and 1945 vanished from Norman's narrative of his life. This silence matters because it was during these years that he developed a good working relationship with the Ila people: when he became warden of the Kafue National Park that helped him overcome challenges which had stymied his predecessor.

There are several other significant omissions. Norman did not write about his time as a game ranger based in Ndola, where his work had little to do with community-based conservation. His Ndola posting culminated with a buffalo goring him which necessitated two major operations and resulted in him having to leave the Game Department. It is possible that he thought potential clients might be discouraged by any mention of serious injuries caused by wild animals. Similarly, he chose not to write about the death of the young girl killed by his lions, Big Boy and Little Boy, in Kafue National Park. This is not to say that her death was a matter of indifference to Norman.

Barbara Carr, Norman's wife, made up for his silence on the child's death by giving the episode a high profile in her book *Not for me the Wilds*. Norman wisely refrained from responding to this or any of the other bitter criticisms levelled at him by Barbara. To have become embroiled in a confrontation in print could only have been counterproductive. Norman chose also to refrain from saying anything about the tensions between him and Peter Hankin, or Peter's short-lived departure for Kenya. To have referred to this in *The Valley of the Elephants* would have been to speak ill of the dead and Norman was too much a gentleman to do any such thing. Instead, he paid tribute to Peter's sterling qualities as a conservationist. Likewise, he preferred not to dwell on the short-termism and profiteering of the main shareholder in Zambia Safaris during the 1980s.

One subject on which his silence is wholly understandable is the incompetence and wastefulness of the Zambian Government under President Kaunda. Professor Andrew Roberts, author of the first comprehensive history of Zambia and later professor of African History at the School of Oriental and African Studies in London, has said in relation to his time at the University of Zambia, that to have been critical of UNIP would have been interpreted as being hostile to Zambia and usually led to expatriates being deported. In addition, Kenneth Kaunda was the only head of government in a newly independent African nation who was genuinely interested in wildlife and supportive of conservation. To have undermined him would have been counterproductive.

Finally, Norman chose not to mention the cottage in Malawi where he did a lot of his reading and writing. His safari business was in Zambia and that was where he wanted tourists to come. So, he wrote as if he spent all his time in the Luangwa Valley. It is intriguing to consider what other significant silences there may be in Norman Carr's publications. No biography is ever wholly complete and there may well be matters that this author knows nothing about.

Endnotes

[1] Gumprich, O. (comp*.) Women in Central Africa.* Mercantile Publishing House: Salisbury. 1930

[2] Bridson, M. 'With the first train into Nyasaland.' *Travel & Exploration* 2(9), 1910, p.179

[3] Carr, N. *The White Impala.* Collins: London. 1969, pp.16-17

[4] Bradley, K. *Once a District Officer.* Macmillan: London. 1966, pp.85-86

[5] Carr, B. *Cherries on my Plate.* Howard Timmins: Cape Town. 1965, p.111

[6] Bradley, K. *Diary of a District Officer.* Thomas Nelson: London. 1947, p.74

[7] Ibid, pp.83-84

[8] Ibid, p.50

[9] Ibid, p.104

[10] Ibid, P.187

[11] Carr, N. *White Impala.* pp.46-47

[12] Carr, B. *The Beastly Wilds.* p.43

[13] Kipling, R. 'Gunga din' in *Barrack Room Ballads.* Methuen: London. 1892. Available online at http://www.kiplingsociety.co.uk/poems_gunga.htm

[14] Carr, B. *Cherries on my Plate.* Howard Timmins: Cape Town. 1965, p.63 and 67

[15] Minutes of meeting of DCs in furthest north districts, 7-9 Aug 1935. NAM S1/207/35

[16] Carr, N. *White Impala.* p.38

[17] Bradley, E. *Dearest Priscilla. Letters to the Wife of a Colonial Civil Servant.* Max Parrish: London. 1950, p.114

[18] Carr, B. *The Beastly Wilds.* p.43

[19] Ibid, p.137

[20] Ibid, p.41

[21] Ibid, pp.74-75

[22] Ibid, p.75

[23] Ibid, p.75

[24] HMSO. *Colonial Annual Reports. Northern Rhodesia, 1946.* London. 1948, p.4

[25] Poles, E. Field Journals, volume 6, pp. 69-70, 11 May 1951, in Library of Zoological Society of London

[26] Boyd, J. M. *Fraser Darling in Africa. A Rhino in the Whistling Thorn.* Edinburgh University Press. 1992, p.18

[27] Ibid, p.36

[28] D. C. Mpika, 'Tour Report No. 5 of 1953,' quoted in Dodds, D. and Patton, D. *Report to the Government of the Republic of Zambia on Wildlife and Land-use survey of the Luangwa Valley.* FAO: Rome. 1968

[29] Carr, N. *White Impala.* p.101

[30] Ibid, pp.176-177. See also Trapnell, C. G. and Clothier, J. N. *Soils, Vegetation and*

Agricultural Systems of North Western Rhodesia. Northern Rhodesia Government Printer: Lusaka. 1937

[31] Ibid, p.124

[32] Zoological Society of London. *Annual Report for 1953.* London. 1954, p.10

[33] Carr, N. *Valley of the Elephants. The Story of the Luangwa Valley and its Wildlife.* Collins: London. 1979, pp.14-16

[34] Bradley, K. *Diary of a District Officer.* Thomas Nelson: London. 1947 edition (first published 1943), pp.86-88

[35] Poles, E. Field Journals, volume 1, p.297, [no day] July 1947

[36] Carr, N. *White Impala,* p.108

[37] Chipungu, S. 'Accumulation from within: the Boma class and the Native Treasury in Colonial Zambia' in Chipungu, S. (ed.) *Guardians in their time. Experiences of Zambians under colonial rule, 1890-1964.* Macmillan: London. 1992, p.83

[38] Boyd, J. M. *Fraser Darling in Africa,* p.88

[39] HMSO, *Colonial Annual Reports. Northern Rhodesia, 1949.* London. 1950, p. 65

[40] Carr, N. 'Elephants in the Eastern Province,' *Northern Rhodesia Journal* 1, 2, 1950, p.25

[41] Ibid, p.25

[42] HMSO, *Colonial Annual Reports. Northern Rhodesia, 1950.* London. 1951, p. 79

[43] HMSO, *Colonial Annual Reports. Northern Rhodesia, 1951.* London. 1952, p. 72

[44] Carr, N. *Valley of the Elephants,* pp.16-17

[45] Government of Northern Rhodesia, Game and Tsetse Control Department, *Annual Report,* 1950, p.3

[46] Fleming, I. *Dr No.* Vintage Books: London. 2012 (first published in 1958), pp.41-42

[47] Carr, N. *White Impala,* p.189

[48] Poles, E. Unpublished Journal, Volume 9, 5 February 1952, in Library of Zoological Society of London

[49] Carr, B. *Cherries on my Plate,* pp.121-122

[50] Carr, B. *The Beastly Wilds,* p. 219

[51] Ibid, pp.223-224

[52] Ibid, p.225

[53] Carr, B. *Cherries on my Plate,* p.128

[54] Game and Tsetse Department. *Annual Report for 1955.* In CO1015/20, The National Archives of the United Kingdom

[55] Manning, I. *With a Gun in Good Country,* p.168

[56] Carr, B. *The Beastly Wilds,* pp.73-75

[57] Northern Rhodesia Government, Government Notice 210, *Proclamation of National Park. Boundaries of Kafue National Park, 1961*

[58] Carr, N. *Return to the Wild.* Collins: London, 1962, pp.23-24

59 Ibid, p.57

60 Ibid, p. 29

61 Carr, N. *The White Impala,* pp.30-33

62 Ibid, p.163

63 Ibid, p.146

64 Attenborough, D. *Life on Air.* BBC Books: London. 2010, p.152

65 Carr, N. *Return to the Wild,* p.124

66 Carr, N. *White Impala,* p.150

67 Attenborough, D. *Life on Air,* p.197

68 Short, R. *African Sunset.* Johnson: Chicago. 1973, pp.196-197

69 Carr, N. *Kakuli.* CBC Publishing: Ontario. 1996, pp.25-26

70 Carr, N. *Valley of the Elephants,* p.19

71 Carr, N. *White Impala,* p.134

72 Carr, N. *Valley of the Elephants,* p.122

73 Carr, N. *Valley of the Elephants,* p.120

74 Roberts, A. *A History of Zambia.* Heinemann: Oxford. 1976, p.232

75 Mwanakatwe, J.M. *End of Kaunda Era.* Multimedia Zambia: Lusaka. 1994, pp.128-129

76 Kelly, D. *Luangwa. Memories of Eden. David Kelly paints South Luangwa National Park.* Published by author, 2004, p.51

77 Dodds, D. and Patton, D. *Report to Government of Republic_of Zambia on Wildlife and Land-use Survey of the_Luangwa Valley.* United Nations Food and Agriculture Organisation: Rome. 1968, p.79

78 Ibid, p.102

79 Ibid,

80 Dunlap, R. C. *Luangwa Valley Conservation and Development Project, Zambia. A Tourism Plan for the Luangwa Valley.* United Nations Food and Agriculture Organisation: Rome. 1973, p.4

81 Hanks, J. *Operation Lock and War on Rhino Poaching.* Penguin: London. 2015, p.9

82 Boyd, R. *Colonial Odyssey.* Navigator Books: Ringwood, Hampshire. 1996, p.101

83 Carr, N. *Kakuli,* pp.149-151

84 Manning, I. *With a Gun in Good Country,* pp.145-146

85 Carr, N. *Valley of the Elephants,* p.23

86 Manning, I. *With a Gun in Good Country,* p.155

87 Ibid, p.73

88 Bradley, K. *Diary of a District Officer.* Nelson: London, 1943

89 Kelly, D. *Luangwa. Memories of Eden,* p.30

90 Guhrs, V. *The Trouble with Africa: Stories from a Safari Camp.* Penguin Books: London. 2004, p.29

[91] Manning, I. *With a Gun in Good Country,* p.257

[92] Shepherd, M. Personal e-mail message to the author, 29 November 2020

[93] Carr, N. *Kakuli,* pp.108-109

[94] Shepherd, D. 'Introduction' in Carr, N. *Kakuli,* p.vi

[95] Guhrs, V. *The Trouble with Africa,* p.39

[96] Ibid, p.138

[97] Ibid, p.87

[98] Carr, N. *Kakuli,* p.141

[99] Ibid, p.174

[100] House, A. *Great Safari. Lives of George and Joy Adamson.* Harper Collins: London. 1995, p.244

[101] Carr, N. *Some Common Trees and Shrubs of the Luangwa Valley.* Wildlife Conservation Society of Zambia: Lusaka. 1978, p.83

[102] Carr, N. *Valley of the Elephants,* p.122

[103] Carr, N. *Guide to the Wildlife of the Luangwa Valley.* Save the Rhino Trust: Lusaka, sponsored by BP Zambia, revised second edition. 1987, p.21

[104] House, A. *Great Safari,* p.357

[105] Selous, F. C. 'Hunting in Central Africa,' *Travel & Exploration* 1, no.2, 1909, p.128

[106] Carr, N. *White Impala,* p.176

[107] Ibid, p.136

[108] Carr, N. *Kakuli,* p.10

[109] Carr, N. *White Impala,* pp.167-168

[110] Ibid p.174

[111] Guhrs, V. *The Trouble with Africa,* p.206

[112] Carr, N. *White Impala,* p.122

[113] Carr, N. J. *Return to the Wild,* p.7

[114] Shepherd, D. 'Introduction' in Carr, N. J. *Kakuli,* p.v

[115] Ibid.

BIBLIOGRAPHY

Archival Sources

The National Archives of the United Kingdom

CO 670/17 Government Gazettes and Ordinances, 1961

CO 795/122 Labour, Copperbelt, 1942

CO 822/321 Game Preservation in Northern Rhodesia, 1952-54

CO 927/627 Game Preservation in Northern Rhodesia, 1955-56

CO 1015/618 Northern Rhodesia, Game and Tsetse Control Department, Annual Reports, 1950-51

CO 1015/20 Possession of firearms by Africans in Northern Rhodesia

CO 1017/200 Conditions and cost of living ... Northern Rhodesia, 1952

National Archives of Malawi

Personal file of Norman J. Carr, reference Appt, 403I (original Secretariat reference 1064) accessed via Records Centre in Zomba

Marriage licences for Zomba District, 1940. Accessed via Records Centre in Zomba

Nyasaland Volunteer Reserve: Application for enlistment forms, surnames C – D. Accessed via Records Centre in Zomba

National Archives of Zambia

Northern Rhodesia / Zambia staff lists

African Lakes Company Records in Glasgow University Archive Services

Staff book, ref UGC193/1/10/2/1, pp.207, 313 and 485

Staff book, number 2, ref UGC193/1/10/2/2, pp.117 and 241

Minute book ref UGC193/1/1/6, 1911-18

Registrar General for England and Wales (Records accessible via Find My Past website)

Zoological Society of London, Library

Poles, E. Field Journals: volumes 1 to 11, 1947-52, manuscript

Annual Report of the Zoological Society, 1953

Personal Communications

Adrian Carr and Judy Carr, 2013

Publications

Government Publications

United Kingdom

Colonial Reports. Northern Rhodesia, 1946-62. HMSO: London, 1947-63

Northern Rhodesia/Zambia

Government of Northern Rhodesia, *Game and Tsetse Control Department, Annual Reports,* Government Printer: Lusaka

Northern Rhodesia, *Ordinance 43 of 1954, Fauna Conservation*

Northern Rhodesia Government, *General Notice 2121*, 30 October 1962 'Professional hunter services for big game safaris'

Books

Baker, C. *A Fine Chest of Medals.* Mpemba Books: Cardiff, 2003

Boyd, J. M. (ed.), *Fraser Darling in Africa: A Rhino in the Whistling Thorn.* Edinburgh University Press: Edinburgh, 1992

Boyd, R. *Colonial Odyssey.* Navigator Books: Ringwood, Hampshire, 1996

Bradley, E. *Dearest Priscilla; Letters to the Wife of a Colonial Civil Servant.* Max Parrish: London, 1950

Bradley, K. *Diary of a District Officer.* Thomas Nelson: London, 1947

Carr, B. *Cherries on my Plate.* Howard Timmins: Cape Town, 1965

Carr, B. *The Beastly Wilds.* Wingate-Baker: London and New York,1969 [published by Howard Timmins, Cape Town, 1963 as *Not for me the Wilds*]

Carr, N. J. *Return to the Wild.* Collins: London, 1962 [re-printed in Readers Union edition, 1963]

Carr, N. J. *The White Impala.* Collins: London, 1969

Carr, N. J. *Some Common Trees and Shrubs of the Luangwa Valley.* Wildlife Conservation Society of Zambia: Lusaka, 1978

Carr, N. J. *The Valley of the Elephants; The Story of the Luangwa Valley and its Wildlife.* Collins: London, 1979

Carr, N. J. *A Guide to the Wildlife of the Luangwa Valley.* Save the Rhino Trust: Lusaka, 1987

Carr, N. J. *Kakuli; A Story about Wild Animals,their Struggle to Survive and the People who live among them.* CBC Publishing: Harare, 1996

Chipungu, S. (ed.) *Guardians in their Time. Experiences of Zambians under Colonial Rule, 1890-1964.* Macmillan: London, 1992

Darling, Sir Frank F. *Wild Life in an African Territory.* Oxford University Press, 1960

Debenham, F. *Nyasaland. The Land of the Lake.* HMSO: London, 1955

Dodds, D. and Patton, D. *Report to the Government of the Republic of Zambia on Wildlife and Land-use Survey of the Luangwa Valley.* FAO: Rome, 1968

Dunlap, R. C. *Luangwa Valley Conservation and Development Project, Zambia. A Tourism Plan for the Luangwa Valley.* United Nations Food and Agriculture Organisation: Rome, 1973

Else, D. *Zambia.* Lonely Planet: Melbourne, 2002

Fraser, G. M. *Quartered Safe Out Here.* Harvill: London, 1993

Guhrs, V. *The Trouble with Africa. Stories from a Safari Camp.* Penguin Books: London, 2004

Gumprich, O. (comp.) *Women in Central Africa.* Mercantile Publishing House: Salisbury, 1930

Hanks, J. *Operation Lock and the War on Rhino Poaching.* Penguin: London, 2015

Hobson, D. *Tales of Zambia.* Zambia Society Trust: London,1996

House, A. *The Great Safari: The Lives of George and Joy Adamson.* Harper Collins: London, 1995

Kelly, D. *Luangwa; Memories of Eden. David Kelly paints South Luangwa National Park.* David Kelly: Liwonde, 2004

Kirk-Greene, A. H. M. *A Biographical Dictionary of the British Colonial Service, 1939-1966.* Hans Zell: London, 1991

Manning, I. P. A. *With a Gun in Good Country.* Trophy Room Books: Agoura CA, 1995

McCracken, J. *A History of Malawi, 1859-1966.* James Currey: Woodbridge, 2013

Morris, K. *Zambian Odyssey, 1958-1998.* Privately published, 2000

Mwanakatwe, J.M. *End of Kaunda Era.* Multimedia Publications: Lusaka, 1994

Nunneley, J. *Tales from the King's African Rifles.* Cassell & Co: London, 1998

Pachai, B. *Malawi: The History of the Nation.* Longman: London, 1973

Philip, Prince, Duke of Edinburgh, *Men, Machines and Sacred Cows.* Hamish Hamilton: London, 1984

Roberts, A. *A History of Zambia.* Heinemann: Oxford, 1976

Ruggles-Brise, C. *Notes on Some Birds of Dar es Salaam.* Jarrold & Sons: Norwich, 1927

Norman Carr

Wavell, A. P. *Other Men's Flowers.* Jonathan Cape: London, 1944

White, G. *Natural History and Antiquities of Selbourne.*The Folio Society: London, 1994

Journal Articles and Chapters in Books

Astle, W. 'History of Wildlife Conservation and Management in mid-Luangwa Valley, Zambia,' in Barringer, T. (ed.) *How Green was our Empire?* Institute of Commonwealth Studies: University of London, 2005

Baker, C. 'The Chinde Concession, 1891-1923,' *The Society of Malawi Journal* 33, 1, 1980

Carr, N. J. 'Elephants in the Eastern Province,' *Northern Rhodesia Journal* 1, 2, 1950

Coe, M. 'A History of Wildlife Conservation and Management in Mid-Luangwa Valley,' *BiologicalConservation* 97, 3, 2001

Leader-Williams, N., Albon, S.D. and Berry, P.S.M. 'Illegal Exploitation of Black Rhinoceros and Elephant Populations: patterns of decline, law enforcement and patrol effort in Luangwa Valley, Zambia,'*Journal of Applied Ecology* 27, 1990

Lee, C. 'Jus soli and jus sanguinis in the colonies.' *Law and History Review* 29, 2, 2011

MacKenzie, J. 'Chivalry, Social Darwinism and Ritualised Killing: the hunting ethos in Central Africa up to 1914,' in Anderson, D. and Grove, R. (eds) *Conservation in Africa: people, politics and practice.* Cambridge University Press: Cambridge, 1987

Tough, A.G. and Lihoma, P. 'The development of recordkeeping systems in the British Empire and Commonwealth, 1870s - 1960s,'*Archives & Manuscripts* 40, 3 2012

Tough, A.G. 'The Nchanga Consolidated Copper Mines Limited (NCCM) Company Archives,' *Zambia Library Association Journal* 11, 1, 1979

Newspapers

Nyasaland Times: Obituary of Ernest Alfred Carr, 5 June 1931, and other articles

Unpublished Secondary Sources

Guilbride, P. D. L. 'Pawpaw picnic,' unpublished account of service in Northern Rhodesia as a veterinary officer, MSS.Afr.s.1315, Oxford University Library Service

MacMillan, II. 'History of the African Lakes Company,' unpublished typescript accessed via Glasgow University Library Archives and Special Collections, reference UGC 193/1/14/14

Mfune, O. 'From fortresses to sustainable development: the changing face of environmental conservation in Africa; the case of Zambia,' Ph.D. thesis, University of Glasgow, 2011

Websites

Bishop, L. 'Bishops in Africa,' n.d. (available at myweb.tiscali.co.uk/ espenett/book1/chapt112.htm)

Clark's College Former Pupils' Association website www.clarkscollege. co.uk/pages/history.php accessed March 2013

Wikipedia. 'East African Campaign (World War II)' Available online at http://en.wikipedia.org/wiki/East_African_Campaign_(World_ War_II)

Norman Carr

INDEX

Notes on index

This is an index to names of people, places, and organisations. The names of safari camps have not been indexed, partly because there was a good deal of duplication in their use.

The names of valleys and other geographical features including towns and cities are indexed under the countries in which they are located.The Zambezi is indexed separately as it flows through several countries.